# HIKING CENTRAL ARIZONA

by

Don R. Kiefer

Cover photo: "Hiking the Horton Creek Trail" by Christine M. Hamel

## CAUTION

Physical hazards may be encountered when visiting the areas described in this book. Land ownerships and road conditions change over the years. Readers should take proper precautions and make local inquiries, as author and publishers cannot accept responsibility for such matters. Arizona Ranger Districts are identified to facilitate inquiries for the most current information.

Printed in the United States of America

2nd Printing © 1998

ISBN #1-885590-08-3

Copyright ©1995 by Golden West Publishers. All rights reserved. This book or any portion thereof, may not be reproduced in any form, except for review purposes, without the written permission of the publisher.

Information in this book is deemed to be authentic and accurate by author and publisher. However, they disclaim any liability incurred in connection with the use of information appearing in this book.

**Golden West Publishers, Inc.**
4113 N. Longview Ave.
Phoenix, AZ 85014, USA
(602) 265-4392

# Dedication

To my son, Monte, and his wife, Julie, who have started their young lives together in the mountains of North Carolina.

May they enjoy as much happiness in their lives together as I have in writing this book.

# Acknowledgements

It is my belief that every author has the help of someone else in creating a book. This book was no exception.

A lot of my help was received from the following:

The many agencies listed in this book under, "Where to obtain more information for trails in this book".

MARICOPA CIVIL DEFENSE & EMERGENCY SERVICES with their excellent survival tips.

*MESA TRIBUNE* for having given me a chance to prove my writing skills.

ROBYN WASSERMAN, Vail, Arizona, who was asked for so much in drawing all my maps, never complaining when finding out that, yes, there's more!

Last but not least, EVELYN LONG, Gilbert, Arizona. She has been both my left and right hands since 1986. My career would not be where it is today without her kindness when preparing my work for the publisher.

I fully realize that this book was a team effort.

Thanks to everyone!

*Don Kiefer*

# Central Trails

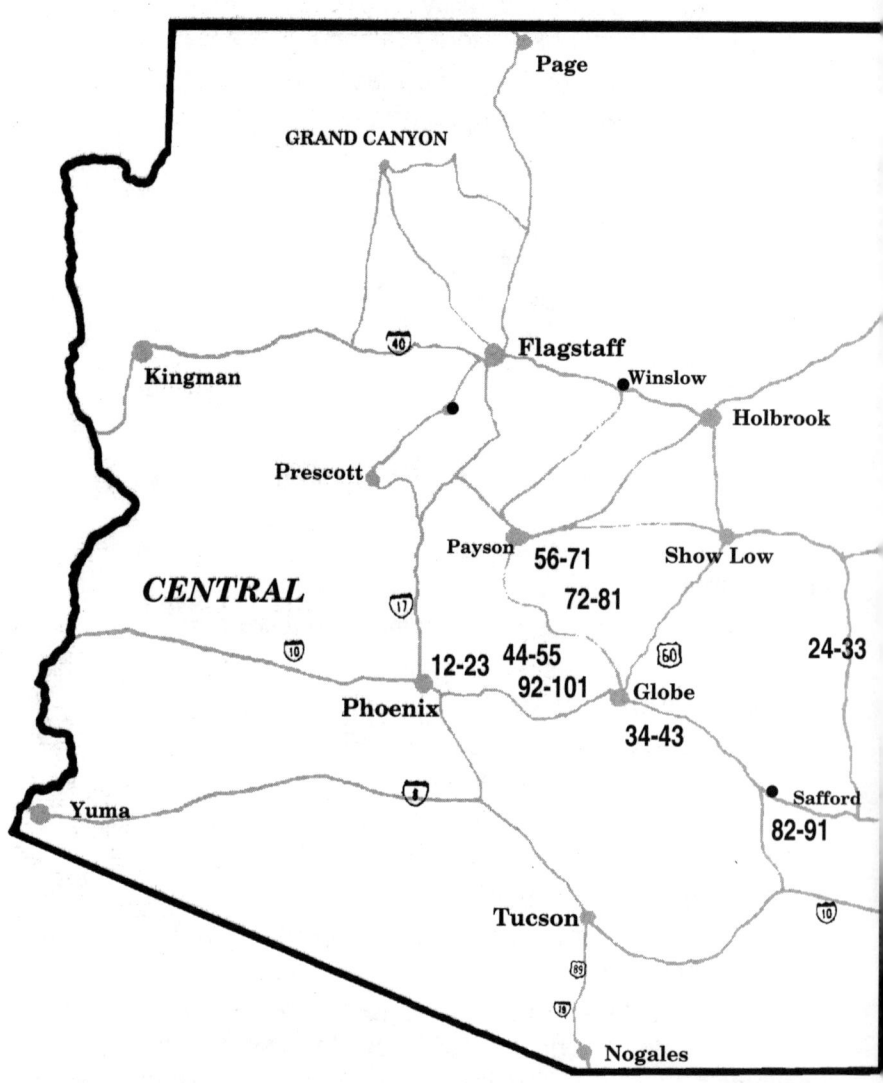

Numbers on map refer to page numbers in book

# Table of Contents

Introduction .................................................................... 7
How to Read the Stat Pages ............................................ 8
Reading Trail Signs ......................................................... 9

## CENTRAL ARIZONA TRAILS

Cave Creek Trail #4 .................................................. 12
Palo Verde Trail #512 ............................................... 14
Quien Sabe Trail #250 .............................................. 16
Skull Mesa Trail #248 ............................................... 20
Skunk Tank Trail #246 .............................................. 22
East Eagle Trail #33 ................................................. 24
Highline Trail #47 ..................................................... 26
Little Blue Creek Trail #41 ........................................ 28
Raspberry Trail #35 .................................................. 30
Strayhorse Canyon Trail #20 .................................... 32
Icehouse Canyon Trail #198 ..................................... 34
Kellner Canyon Trail #242 ........................................ 36
Sixshooter Canyon Trail #197 .................................. 38
Squaw Spring Trail #196 .......................................... 40
Telephone Trail #192 ............................................... 42
Amethyst Trail #253 ................................................. 44
Brown's Trail #133 ................................................... 46
Four Peaks Trail #130 .............................................. 48
Peralta Trail #102 ..................................................... 52
Pigeon Trail #134 ..................................................... 54
Babe Haught Trail #143 ........................................... 56
Highline Trail #31 ..................................................... 58
Horton Creek Trail #285 ........................................... 62
Pine Canyon Trail #26 .............................................. 66
See Canyon Trail #184 ............................................. 70
Abbey's Way Trail #151 ........................................... 72
Dan's Trail #550 ....................................................... 74
Murphy Ranch Trail #141 ......................................... 76
Parker Creek Trail #160 ........................................... 78
Rim Trail #139 .......................................................... 80
Bear Canyon Trail #299 ........................................... 82

(Continued on next page)

(Table of Contents continued from previous page)

    Frye Canyon Trail #36 .................................................. 84
    Grant Goudy Ridge Trail #310 ................................... 86
    Ladybug Trail #329 ...................................................... 88
    Shake Trail #309 .......................................................... 90
    Black Mesa Trail #241 ................................................. 92
    Dutchman's Trail #104 ................................................ 94
    Jug Trail #61 ................................................................ 96
    Reavis Gap Trail #117 ................................................. 98
    Tule Canyon Trail #122 ............................................. 100
Central Arizona Ranger Districts ............................................ 102
Weather—Great, but Changeable ......................................... 103
Trail Etiquette ............................................................................ 104
Contents of Your Day Pack ..................................................... 105
Contents of your Backpack ..................................................... 105
What to Wear for Mountain Hiking ......................................... 106
What to do When You are Lost or Injured ............................. 107
Coping with Hypothermia ........................................................ 108
Safety Rules for Survival in the Desert ................................. 109
Index ........................................................................................... 114
About the Artist ......................................................................... 116
About the Author ...................................................................... 117

## Hiking Tips from the Author

    • Be sure that you have the appropriate topographic maps, and bring this book along too! You may find some of the information included here of lifesaving value!

    • If possible, include a cellular phone in your camping equipment—they have proven invaluable on many occasions.

    • Use the "buddy system" whenever possible. A friend in need is a friend indeed!

    • Always leave information with someone as to where you are going and how long you expect to be gone and remember . . . that information is of no value to anyone if you do not follow your original plans.

    • Be sure to check that you have the Day Pack and Backpack items listed on page 98 as your hike requires.

    • Check the weather forecast before you leave on your hike.

# Introduction

ARIZONA! What would it be like to hike it all? We will never know; one's life span was not designed to allow enough time for any one man or woman to accomplish this.

This book which is part of a new hiking Arizona series *(Hiking Northern Arizona, Hiking Central Arizona,* and *Hiking Southern Arizona)* will provide you with the tools, if used properly, to move you closer to having "hiked it all."

Get ready to either enjoy, or tolerate, the lowland deserts. They make up an area soft with fresh scents, the gentle buzzing of the bees and the silent wanderings of the butterflies. The desert's other side is the extreme heat, many venomous creatures, and storms more vicious than you can imagine.

Also prepare yourself for high altitudes and, yes, even true tundra conditions right here in Arizona. There are areas so quiet you will think you have lost your hearing, with visibility beyond what you thought you could ever see, and so remote you will wonder if there is a way home. Of course, the other extreme exists here as well: snowstorms any day of the year, so much static electricity in the air that your clothes will crack with each step, making it sound as if you are walking on potato chips, 50 m.p.h. winds—Mother Nature on a bad day—and creatures that outweigh you by three and four times that hopefully just watch you go by.

Always thoroughly acquaint yourself with the trail you wish to hike, obtain and study the maps required and, most of all, know and obey your own limitations.

Please be aware that due to funding cutbacks many of Arizona's trails are not in the condition we would like to find them. Currently, volunteers are needed to assist trail maintenance crews. If you would like to aid in this work, please contact the trail managing agency of your choice.

*Don Kiefer*

As you read this book, you may wonder why some of the other major trails in Arizona are not included. The reason is that they are included in my two previous books, *Hiking Arizona* and *Hiking Arizona II*.—D.K.

# HOW TO READ THE STAT PAGES

**ATTRACTION:** Self-explanatory

**REQUIREMENTS:** These are things that cannot be stressed enough. Study the contents of your day packs and backpacks.

**LOCATION:** This is the general area; your maps will do the rest.

**DIFFICULTY:** This will vary with different people; if anything, some are overrated.

**ELEVATIONS:** Most elevations are approximate, but close.

**LENGTH:** Most mileages are approximate, but close.

**MAPS REQUIRED:** Although I have listed the proper topo maps, you must be aware that all trails are not on these maps, but contour lines and altitudes are. You must use the proper Forest Service maps for the corresponding areas. These have not only the trails but roads as well. You can find both maps at good map stores or the proper ranger stations.

**PERMIT:** Although most districts do not require a permit for you to hike, permits are needed for large groups or special activities. You must check with the appropriate agencies to be sure.

**BIKES:** Never permitted in a wilderness area or where posted. I have indicated "No" on a lot of trails simply because bike riding would be very impractical.

**EQUESTRIAN:** Horses are allowed on most trails, but you must study your altitudes and grades and be sure your horse is able to safely negotiate them.

**WATER:** Even though I have said "Yes" on many trails, I have still recommended that you bring your own water. It's always best to drink water you are used to.

**INFORMATION:** These are usually points to be stressed or helpful tips.

**FIREARMS:** When I say "Yes" on firearms, it does not mean you need one, rather that you may carry one if you choose. I have never had any use for one in all my hiking experience, and certainly would not like the extra weight.

**PETS:** Although pets are not strictly forbidden on most Forest Service trails, you still have many responsibilities. **Your pet is to be contained.** Your pet is to be very obedient or on a leash. Your pet must not be permitted to chase wildlife or to scare others on foot or horseback.

**TRAIL INFORMATION:** This will contain directions to trailheads along with the trail information itself.

*All of the above information is to be thoroughly studied before ever setting foot on a trail if you are to have a good hike.*

# Reading Trail Signs

"How elementary!" you may say. When you come upon a sign that reads, "Peach Springs - 2.5 miles," how hard can it be to understand? Let's consider this, however. You get caught in a snowstorm and it dumps about four inches of snow and the terrain becomes level (it happened to me). Except for distance, the above trail sign is of no more value; it is obvious that you need to look for other trail signs besides a post and a board.

## 1. Chevrons

Chevrons are metal tabs about three inches square, that are tacked to trees along the trail about six to eight feet above the ground. The ones I have seen have been white, orange or red. You must be careful not to lose sight of the one you just passed before the next one comes into view. Some trees will have two chevrons indicating either that another trail connects the trail you are on, or that there is a very sharp turn in your trail. Take a minute to study the area well when two chevrons are encountered. Chevrons are found mostly in high altitudes.

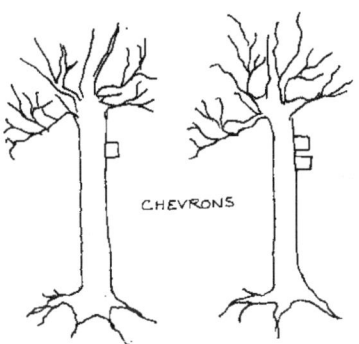

## 2. Tree Notches

These notches are carved into trees at about the five to six-foot level. Most are about 3/4 inch deep and have rounded edges because of the tree's ability to eventually heal over the notch. They are a little harder to spot as they take on the same color as the tree. Notches sometimes are found in the lower altitudes as well. They are interpreted exactly the same as chevrons.

### 3. Cairns

Cairns are very expertly arranged stacks of rocks along the trail, graduating from a large base to almost a point. I have seen them from ten inches high to four feet high, and they simply guide your way. These are found on areas of trails that are just rock surfaces, where a path will never be worn and there are no trees for chevrons or notches. Believe me, it's a very hit-and-miss situation getting through areas like this without a scattering of rock cairns.

As you can see, trail signs come in many forms and it is a good idea to train yourself to spot them, even though you may not be having any problems finding your way.

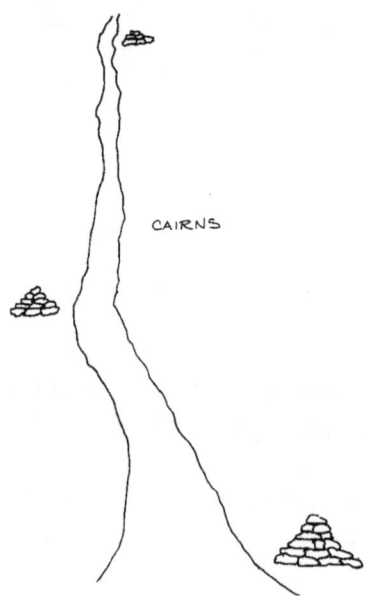

# Hiking Central Arizona

# CAVE CREEK TRAIL #4

**ATTRACTION:** Ease of travel; home of the Gila Topminnow (an endangered species); other trail options.

**REQUIREMENTS:** Lots of water, food, sturdy boots, proper maps; car okay to Cave Creek trailhead; high clearance vehicle needed to Spur Cross trailhead; 4.5 hours hiking time one way.

**LOCATION:** Cave Creek Ranger Dist., Seven Springs Rec. Area.

**DIFFICULTY:** Easy       **ELEVATIONS:** 3360' - 2840' - 2600'

**LENGTH:** 10.1 miles one way.

**MAPS REQUIRED:** U.S.G.S. 7.5 min. topographic quads for New River Mesa and Humboldt Mountain; Tonto National Forest map; Cave Creek Trail System map.

**PERMIT:** No       **BIKES:** Yes       **EQUESTRIAN:** Yes

**WATER:** Yes - best to bring your own or purify.

**INFORMATION:** Cave Creek Horsemen's Association adopted this trail. Watch for rattlesnakes.

**FIREARMS:** Yes       **PETS ON LEASH:** Yes

## TRAIL INFORMATION

Take Cave Creek Road approximately 18 miles northeast from Carefree to Cave Creek trailhead, just past Seven Springs Campground; trailhead will be on left.

From trailhead, the trail stays close to Cave Creek, crossing it several times. From Matty's Fork wash to the Spur Cross trailhead, the trail remains elevated and out of the riparian area. From Cave Creek trailhead in the Seven Springs Recreation Area, the trail goes south, with a short spur leading to CCC Campground. Half a mile from the trailhead, the trail crosses FR 24B and turns west. After half a mile, the junction with Cottonwood Trail #247 occurs, then the trail passes Ashdale Admin. Site (Forest Service work area). After three stream crossings is the junction with Quien Sabe Trail #250. After two more stream crossings, the trail crosses Matty's Fork Wash. From there the trail climbs 300 ft. and stays along the slope, crossing Chalk Canyon, and ending at FR 1533. Following FR 1533 south about .4 mile takes you past the west end of Cottonwood Trail #247 and on to Spur Cross Road (FR 48).

# CAVE CREEK TRAIL #4

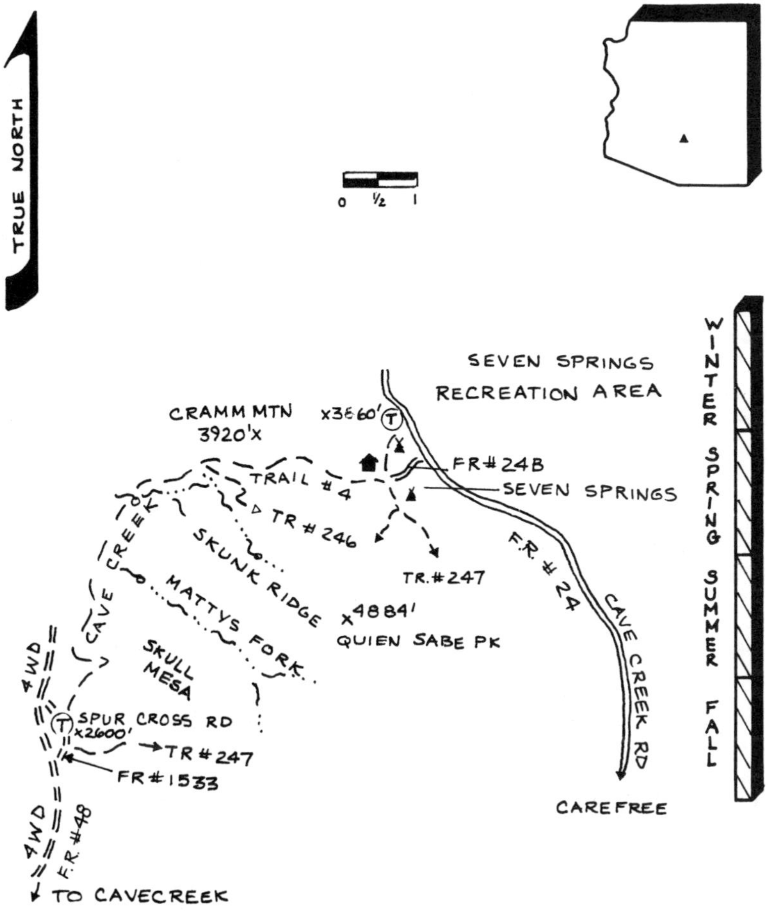

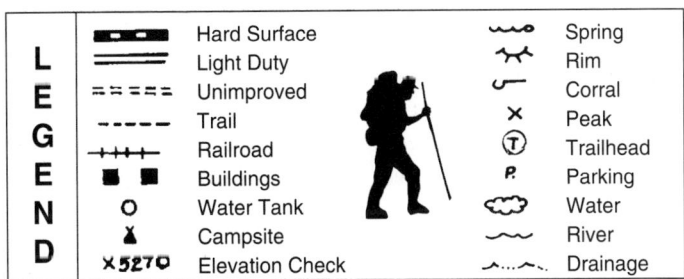

Hiking Central Arizona / 13

# PALO VERDE TRAIL #512

**ATTRACTION:** Views of Bartlett Lake; fine examples of saguaro cactus, mesquite, palo verde and ironwood trees.

**REQUIREMENTS:** Lots of water, food, sturdy boots, proper maps; car okay to trailhead; 2 hours hiking time one way.

**LOCATION:** Cave Creek Ranger District, 20 mi. east of Carefree.

**DIFFICULTY:** Easy

**ELEVATIONS:** 1820' - 1840'

**LENGTH:** 4 miles one way.

**MAPS REQUIRED:** U.S.G.S. 7.5 min. topographic for Bartlett Dam - Maverick Mountain.

**PERMIT:** No

**BIKES:** Yes          **EQUESTRIAN:** No

**WATER:** Yes - best to bring your own.

**INFORMATION:** Motorized access to Rattlesnake Cove will not be open; check with District Ranger for update.

**FIREARMS:** Yes          **PETS ON LEASH:** Yes

## TRAIL INFORMATION

Trail starting points are on the north side of Rattlesnake Cove and the south side of SB Cove in the Bartlett Lake Recreation Area. The recreation area is reached by following Cave Creek Road 7 miles east of Carefree to junction with Forest Road 205. Turn right and travel 6 miles to junction with Forest Road 19. Take Forest Road 19 for nearly 7 miles to junction with Forest Road 459, then Forest Road 459 to the turnoff for Rattlesnake Cove, or continue to SB Cove. Only the last mile is unpaved.

The south end of the trail begins near the northern edge of Rattlesnake Cove Recreation Site. Trail parallels shoreline of Bartlett Reservoir, providing access to the shore, crossing washes and small ridges, and running along hill slopes. From Rattlesnake Cove trailhead to SB Cove is 2.5 miles. A 1.5 mile loop trail intersects the main trail at two locations: about .1 mile south of SB Cove and again .5 mile south of SB Cove. The loop trail provides access to additional areas near the edge of the lake.

# PALO VERDE TRAIL #512

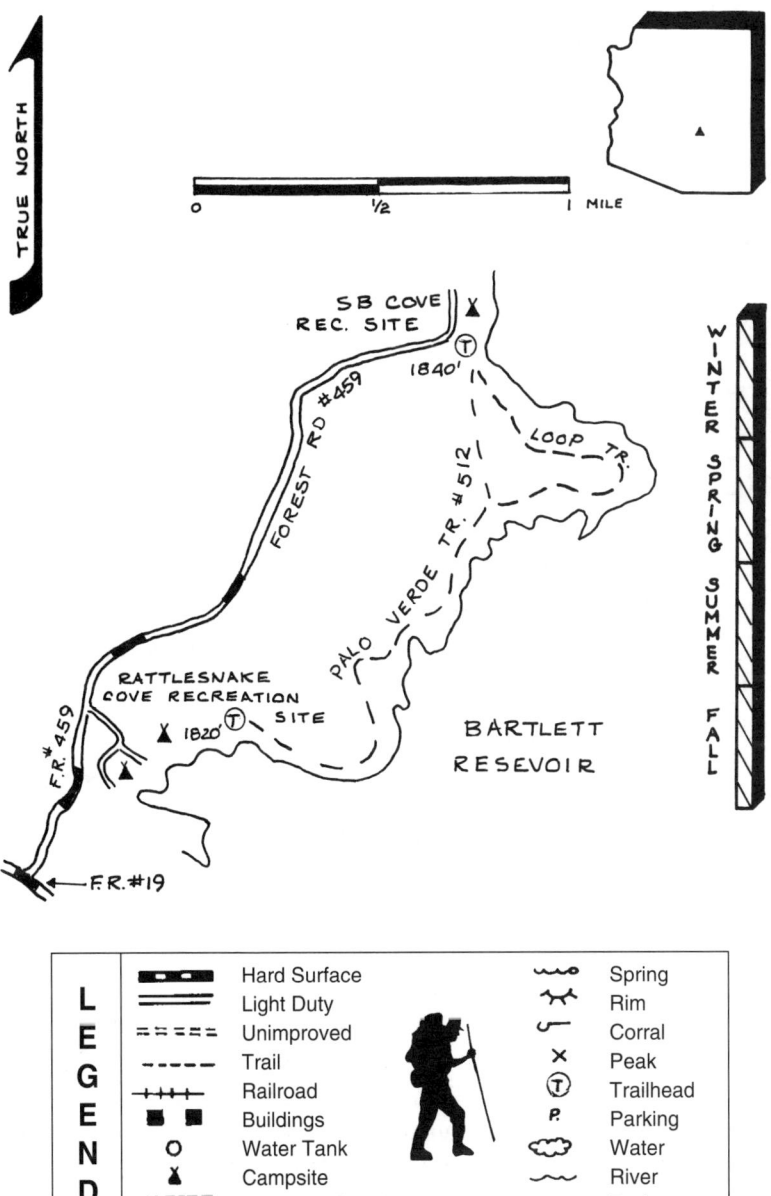

*Hiking Central Arizona* / 15

# QUIEN SABE TRAIL #250

**ATTRACTION:** Travels through the heart of this trail system, including a prescribed burn in 1993.

**REQUIREMENTS:** Lots of water, food, sturdy boots, proper maps; car okay to trailhead on Forest Road 24 access only; 4-wheel drive needed on Forest Road 48 if open; 4 hours total hiking time.

**LOCATION:** Cave Creek Ranger District, north of Cave Creek and Carefree.

**DIFFICULTY:** Easy

**ELEVATIONS:** 3800' - 4080'

**LENGTH:** 2.5 miles one way.

**MAPS REQUIRED:** U.S.G.S. 7.5 min. topographic for New River Mesa.

**PERMIT:** No

**BIKES:** No

**EQUESTRIAN:** Yes

**WATER:** Yes - best to bring your own.

**INFORMATION:** Campground is not the trailhead; trail users should park at Cave Creek trailhead .2 mile north of CCC Campground.

**FIREARMS:** Yes

**PETS ON LEASH:** Yes

## TRAIL INFORMATION

Take Cave Creek Road approximately 18 miles northeast from Carefree to Cave Creek trailhead, just past Seven Springs Campground. Trailhead will be on the left.

Quien Sabe Trail is in the center of the Cave Creek Trail System, connecting Skunk Tank Trail #246 to Skull Mesa Trail #248. Access is from Cave Creek trailhead in the Seven Springs Recreation Area on Forest Road 24, or from Spur Cross trailhead on Forest Road 48. From Cave Creek trailhead, follow Cave Creek Trail #4. In .5 mile, cross Forest Road 24B, and .5 mile further is

(Continued on Page 18)

# QUIEN SABE TRAIL #250

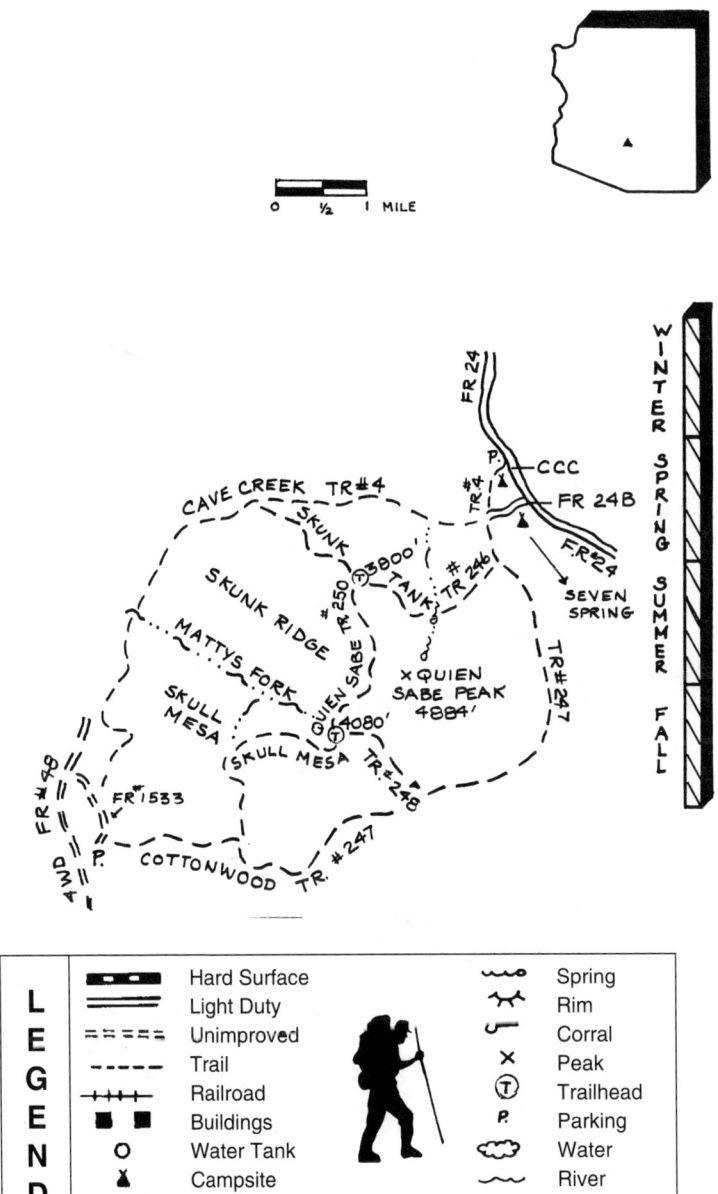

(Continued from Page 16)

the junction with Cottonwood Trail #247. Take Cottonwood Trail .5 mile to junction with Skunk Tank Trail; take Skunk Tank Trail. Climb 600 ft. over 2.5 miles, past Quien Sabe Spring, and go to junction with Quien Sabe Trail #250, at 4080 ft. elevation. Quien Sabe Trail climbs to the divide between Skunk Tank Canyon and Matty's Fork drainages at 4400 ft. The trail drops 600 ft. to the head of Matty's Fork drainage, then climbs to junction with Skull Mesa Trail. Follow Skull Mesa Trail west, climbing 500 ft. to the top of the Mesa. Follow rock cairns across the grassy mesa. Descend 1000 ft. in less than a mile with numerous switchbacks. At junction with Cottonwood Trail, proceed west 2 miles to junction with Forest Road 1533. Follow Forest Road 1533 .2 mile west to junction with Spur Cross Road 48 at Spur Cross trailhead.

*You will see many saguaros along the Skull Mesa Trail. Notice the crested saguaro on the left.*
*(Photo by John Villinski)*

Skull Mesa Trail.
(Photo by John Villinski)

Spiral petroglyph symbol for "water" or "stream" near Cottonwood Creek.
(Photo by John Villinski)

Skull Mesa Trail—worth the effort!
(Photo by Christine M. Hamel)

# SKULL MESA TRAIL #248

**ATTRACTION:** Panoramic view of desert foothills.
**REQUIREMENTS:** Lots of water, food, sturdy boots, proper maps; car okay to trailhead on F.R. 24; 5 hours hiking time.
**LOCATION:** Cave Creek Ranger District. North of Cave Creek.
**DIFFICULTY:** Very difficult
**ELEVATIONS:** 3260' - 4560'
**LENGTH:** 3 miles one way
**MAPS REQUIRED:** U.S.G.S. 7.5 min. topographic for New River Mesa.
**PERMIT:** No  **BIKES:** No
**EQUESTRIAN:** Yes
**WATER:** Yes - best to bring your own.
**INFORMATION:** Check access on F.R. 48 - 4-wheel drive only.
**FIREARMS:** Yes  **PETS ON LEASH:** Yes

## TRAIL INFORMATION

Take Cave Creek Road approximately 18 miles northeast from Carefree to Cave Creek trailhead, just past Seven Springs campground. Trailhead will be on left. This trail is accessible from Cottonwood Trail #247, starting at the Spur Cross trailhead, or from Quien Sabe Trail #250, starting at Cave Creek trailhead in the Seven Springs Recreation area.

From Spur Cross trailhead, follow F.R. 1533 for .2 mile to the start of Cottonwood Trail. Follow Cottonwood Trail 2 miles to the west junction with Skull Mesa Trail #248. Take Skull Mesa Trail up numerous switchbacks, gaining over 1000 ft. in less than a mile. At the edge of the mesa, follow rock cairns across the grassland, reaching the highest elevation of 4560'. Descend 500 ft. to Quien Sabe Trail junction. Continue on Skull Mesa Trail, descending 400 ft. to Cottonwood Trail junction in Cottonwood Creek drainage. Cottonwood Trail west takes you out of the drainage and about 3 miles to west junction with Skull Mesa Trail. On Cottonwood Trail, retrace route to Spur Cross trailhead (FR 48). Cottonwood Creek is intermittent but several permanent springs are near the trail. Loop trip described is about 8 to 9 miles.

# SKULL MESA TRAIL #248

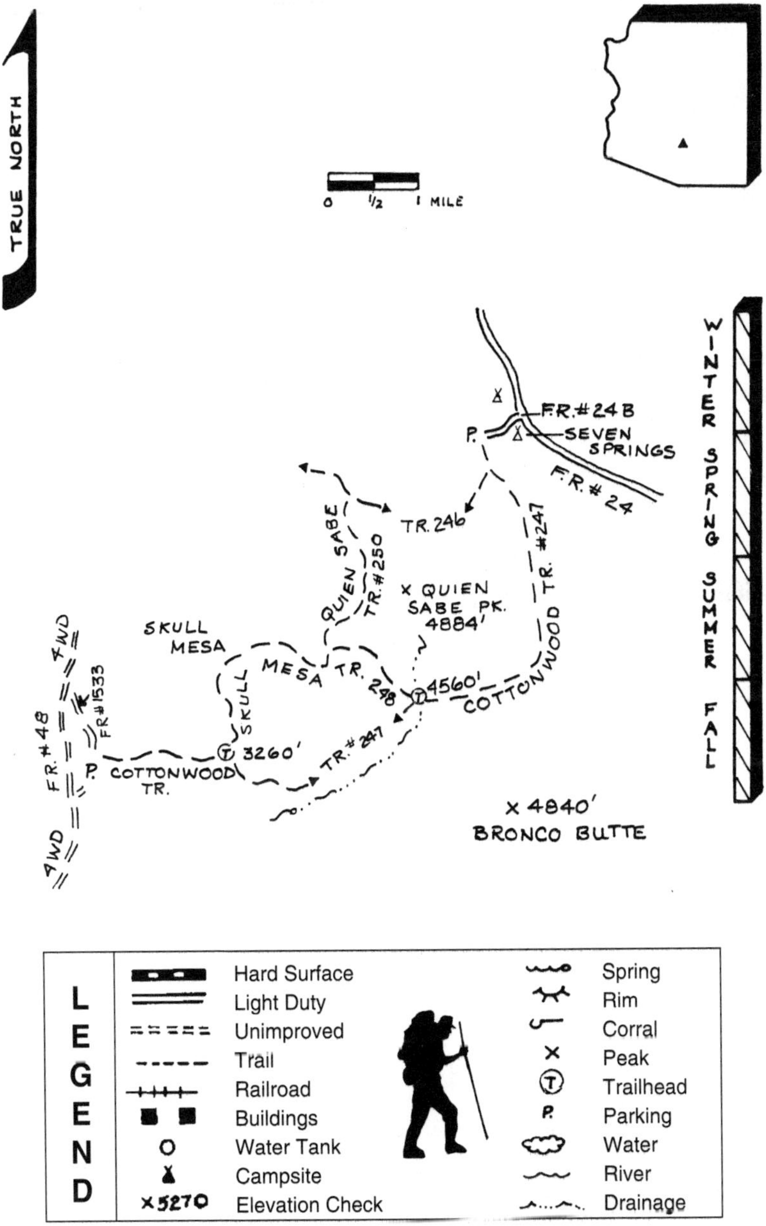

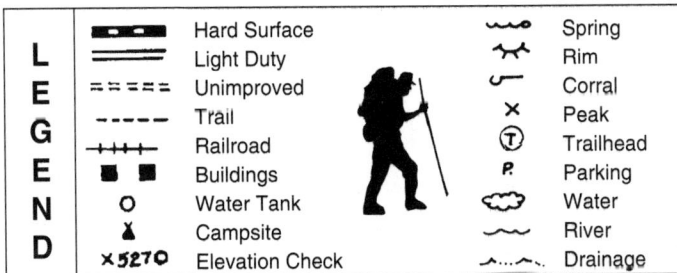

Hiking Central Arizona / 21

# SKUNK TANK TRAIL #246

**ATTRACTION:** Dramatic views of Skunk Tank Canyon, Cave Creek drainage, and Cramm Mountain mining operation.

**REQUIREMENTS:** Water, food, sturdy boots, proper maps; car okay to trailhead; 4 to 6 hours round trip, depending on which route is taken.

**LOCATION:** Cave Creek Ranger Dist., Seven Springs Rec. Area.

**DIFFICULTY:** Moderate to Difficult

**ELEVATIONS:** 3440' - 4080' - 2920'

**LENGTH:** 4.8 miles one way or 11-mile loop

**MAPS REQUIRED:** U.S.G.S. 7.5 min. topographic for Humboldt Mountain and New River Mesa; Tonto National Forest map; Cave Creek Trails System map.

**PERMIT:** No          **BIKES:** No

**EQUESTRIAN:** Yes     **WATER:** Not dependable

**INFORMATION:** Trail served as northern boundary of Quien Sabe prescribed burn in June 1993. FR 24 can be impassable during spring runoff. Watch for rattlesnakes.

**FIREARMS:** Yes       **PETS ON LEASH:** Yes

## TRAIL INFORMATION

Take Cave Creek Road approximately 18 miles northeast from Carefree to Cave Creek trailhead, just past Seven Springs campground. Trailhead will be on the left.

Skunk Tank Trail #246 is accessible from Cave Creek Trail #4 starting at Cave Creek trailhead in the Seven Springs Rec. Area. A good 11-mile loop trip starts on Cave Creek Trail #4, which crosses FR 24B after half a mile. Another half mile later, Trail #4 goes to the junction with Cottonwood Trail #247. Take Cottonwood Trail half a mile to the junction with Skunk Tank Trail, then follow Skunk Tank Trail. Climb about 600 feet for about 2.5 miles, past Quien Sabe Spring, and go to the junction with Quien Sabe Trail #250. This is the highest point. The next 2.3 miles, pass Skunk Tank (a reservoir for cattle which also attracts deer), and descend about 1160 feet along Skunk Tank Canyon to Cave Creek and Cave Creek Trail #4.

# SKUNK TANK TRAIL #246

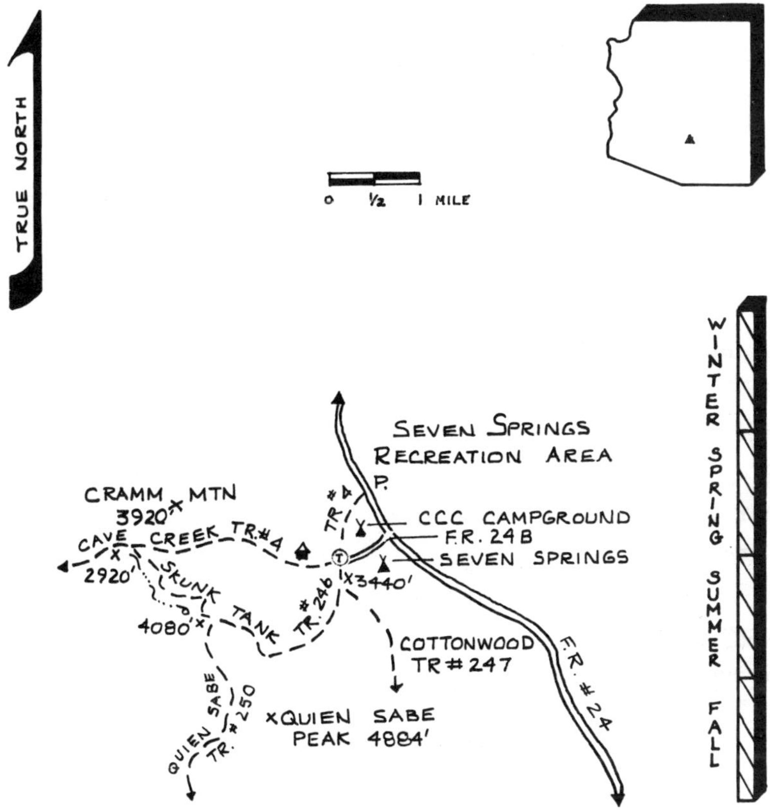

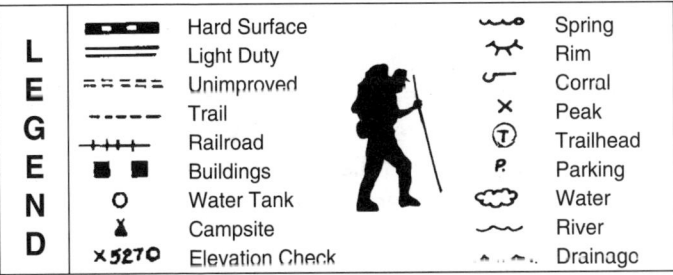

*Hiking Central Arizona* / 23

# EAST EAGLE TRAIL #33

**ATTRACTION:** Wildlife, solitude, scenery.

**REQUIREMENTS:** Food, water, sturdy boots, proper maps; car okay to trailhead; 5.5 hours hiking time one way.

**LOCATION:** Clifton Ranger District - connects U.S. 191 with Eagle Creek Road.

**DIFFICULTY:** Difficult

**ELEVATIONS:** 7200' - 5850'

**LENGTH:** 13.5 miles one way

**MAPS REQUIRED:** U.S.G.S. 7.5 min. topographic for Hannagan Meadow and Morenci.

**PERMIT:** No

**BIKES:** Not recommended

**EQUESTRIAN:** Yes

**WATER:** Not dependable - bring your own.

**INFORMATION:** Have a plan for the end of this hike, either to stay overnight or take a shuttle back.

**FIREARMS:** Yes

**PETS ON LEASH:** Yes - on leash or controlled.

## TRAIL INFORMATION

Trailhead can be found on U.S. 191 approximately 27.5 miles south of Alpine, shortly after Strayhorse Campground on the right.

From an altitude of 7200', the trail heads due west and slightly to the south for approximately 5 miles to its junction with Crabtree Trail #22. At this point, you will have dropped about 1200 feet in elevation. In 3 more miles, Hot Air Trail #15 heads to the south. In only 1/4 mile from this location will be the junction with Salthouse Trail #18 that heads northeast. East Eagle Trail now will become an old jeep road that will intersect with Dry Prong Creek and Eagle Canyon in just about 4 more miles. The trail will end in only 2 more miles at the junction with Eagle Creek Road #217.

Study your maps.

# EAST EAGLE TRAIL #33

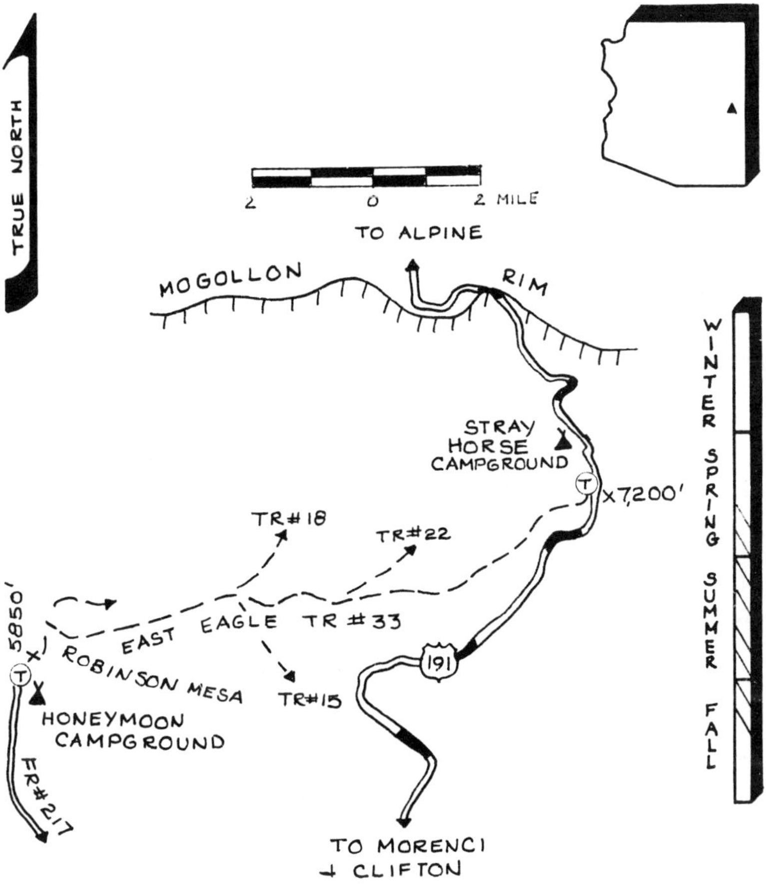

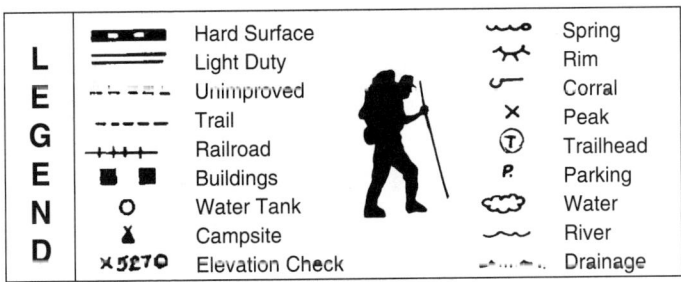

Hiking Central Arizona / 25

# HIGHLINE TRAIL #47

**ATTRACTION:** Big game animals, smaller mammals, many birds, turkeys, wildflowers.

**REQUIREMENTS:** Food, water, sturdy boots, proper maps; car okay to trailhead; 6 hours hiking time one way.

**LOCATION:** Clifton Ranger District, west of Strayhorse Campground.

**DIFFICULTY:** Difficult

**ELEVATIONS:** 7600' - 7000'

**LENGTH:** 14.6 miles one way.

**MAPS REQUIRED:** U.S.G.S. 7.5 min. topographic for Hannagan Meadow and Morenci.

**PERMIT:** No

**BIKES:** Not recommended

**EQUESTRIAN:** Yes

**WATER:** Yes but best to bring your own.

**INFORMATION:** Be aware of cattle sharing the area. Have plans when trail is completed.

**FIREARMS:** Yes    **PETS ON LEASH:** Yes, or controlled

## TRAIL INFORMATION

Trailhead is at Strayhorse Campground which can be found 26 miles south of Alpine on U.S. 191.

Trail travels west out of campground for one mile to East Eagle Creek. At 1.4 miles will be the junction with Crabtree Trail #22, and then Crabtree Creek in .1 mile more. At about 2.4 miles, you will travel through the Salthouse Fire area of 1959. At 3.5 miles are cabin ruins on the bottom of Salthouse Creek, and the junction of Salthouse Trail #18. The junction of Chitty Trail #37 at the bottom of Chitty Creek will be reached at mile 6.7. At 8 miles is the junction of McBride Mesa Trail #26 and Helispot 166 and Helispot 167 at mile 9.8. At 10.7 miles is the junction with the road to Saunders cabin. The actual cabin is at mile 11.1, as well as the junction with Squirrel Trail #34. The trail ends at junction with Dry Prong Trail #45.

# HIGHLINE TRAIL #47

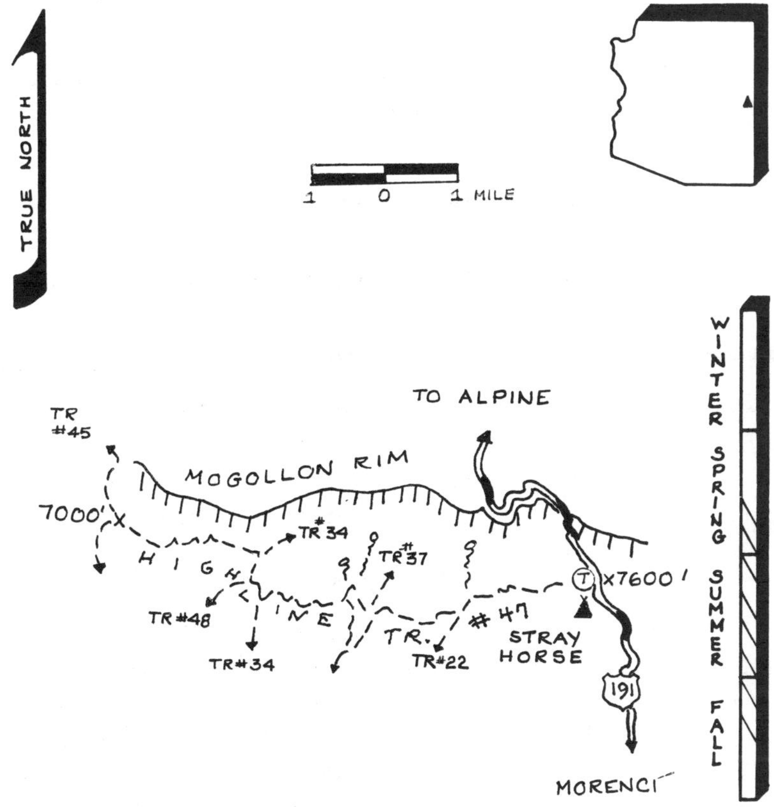

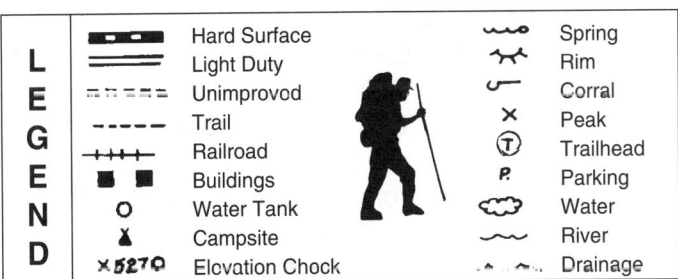

*Hiking Central Arizona* / 27

# LITTLE BLUE CREEK TRAIL #41

**ATTRACTION:** Wildlife, scenery, nice views.

**REQUIREMENTS:** Food, water, sturdy boots, proper maps; pickup, jeep or 4-wheel drive only to trailhead; 4.5 hours hiking time one way.

**LOCATION:** Clifton Ranger District - New Mexico State Line northeast through Bear Valley area.

**DIFFICULTY:** Difficult

**ELEVATIONS:** 6000' - 6800' - 7800'

**LENGTH:** 10.7 miles one way

**MAPS REQUIRED:** U.S.G.S. 7.5 min. topographic for Alma Mesa Blue SW-Blue SE.

**PERMIT:** No             **BIKES:** No, wilderness area

**EQUESTRIAN:** Yes        **WATER:** Yes - purify

**INFORMATION:** Have a plan for end of trail, and remember it ends in Alpine Ranger District if more information is needed.

**FIREARMS:** Yes          **PETS ON LEASH:** Yes

## TRAIL INFORMATION

Take State Route 180 north out of Glenwood, New Mexico about 5 miles to Alma, and then turn left on Forest Road #106. In 1/4 mile, you will cross the San Francisco River. At this point, turn north on Forest Road #104 and continue for 7 miles to Forest Road #711. Take Forest Road #711 for about 4 miles east to the state line and trailhead. Trailhead is not marked so stay alert.

Begin trail at 6000' at the New Mexico state line fence and gate. At the 1-mile mark you will again encounter the state line, where there is a cabin, well and corral. For the next 3 miles it will be a steady climb to 6800'. At 5.5 miles will be the junction with Yam Canyon and Little Blue Creek, at which point you will have descended to 6200'. At 7 miles the canyon forks, and in .9 mile more will be a junction with Bear Valley Trail #55, entering Bear Valley. At 10.2 miles the trail will leave Little Blue Creek, and at 10.7 miles will be the junction with Campbell Flat Trail #54 in the Alpine Ranger District, at 7800 feet.

# LITTLE BLUE CREEK TRAIL #41

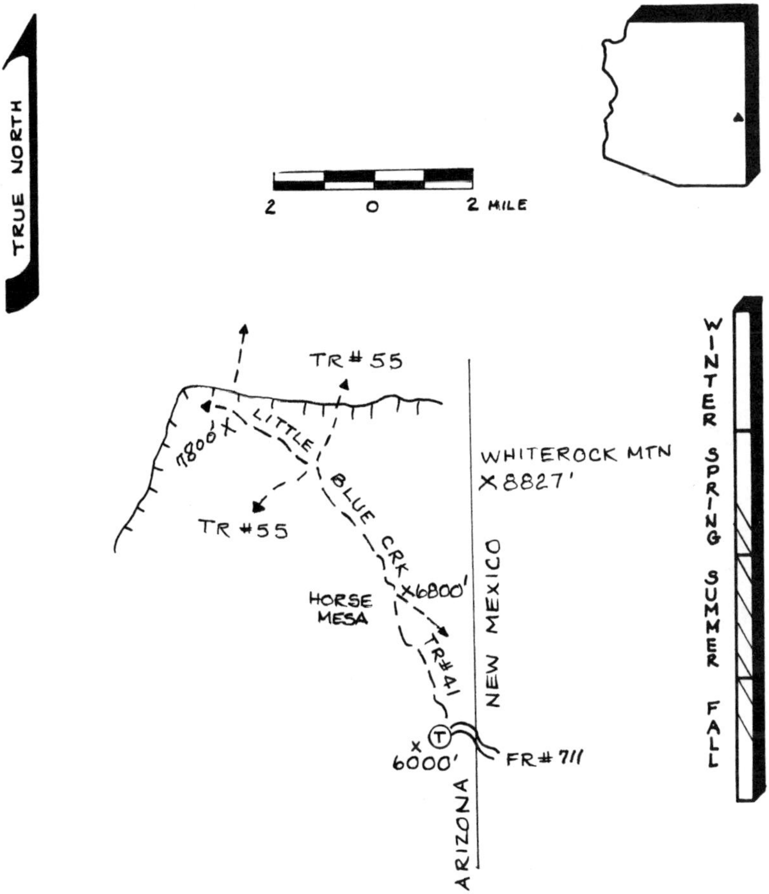

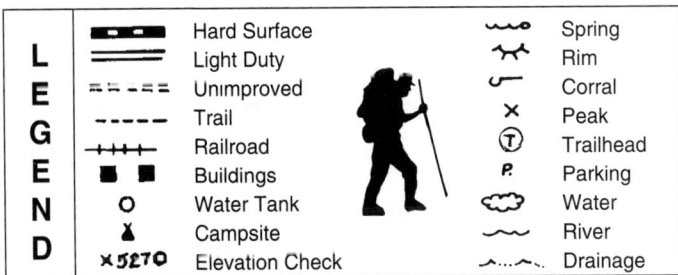

# RASPBERRY TRAIL #35

**ATTRACTION:** Trail travels from ponderosa pine to cottonwoods; wild turkeys and many songbirds found on this trail.

**REQUIREMENTS:** Food, water, sturdy boots, proper maps; car okay to Strayhorse Campground; jeep or walk last 1/4 mile to trailhead; 4.5 hours hiking time one way.

**LOCATION:** Clifton Ranger District - Blue Ridge Primitive Area.

**DIFFICULTY:** Difficult

**ELEVATIONS:** 7600' - 5100'

**LENGTH:** 10.5 miles one way

**MAPS REQUIRED:** U.S.G.S. 7.5 min. topographic for Hannagan Meadow S.E.-Blue S.W.

**PERMIT:** No

**BIKES:** No

**EQUESTRIAN:** Yes

**WATER:** Yes - treat or bring your own.

**INFORMATION:** A car shuttle at end of trail would work well to avoid the long hike back uphill.

**FIREARMS:** Yes          **PETS ON LEASH:** Yes

## TRAIL INFORMATION

Strayhorse Campground can be found 26 miles south of Alpine on U.S. 191.

Trail begins at the Rattlesnake Ranch which is 1/4 mile east of Strayhorse Campground, via a jeep road. As the trail descends it enters the Blue Ridge Primitive Area at about 2.5 miles where, of course, no motorized travel is permitted. Trail is easy to follow as it follows Raspberry Creek. At 4 miles you leave Clifton Ranger District and enter Alpine Ranger District. At 6 miles and at 5600' you will leave the creek bed and climb back to 5800'. At 7 miles you will again descend towards the creek and actually enter it at 9.5 miles, at an altitude of 5200'. Trail ends in 1 mile at Forest Road #281 at the Blue River, at 5100'. Forest Road #281 continues north to U.S. 180 near Alpine. It also follows the Blue River south for another mile where it ends and the Blue River Trail begins.

# RASPBERRY TRAIL #35

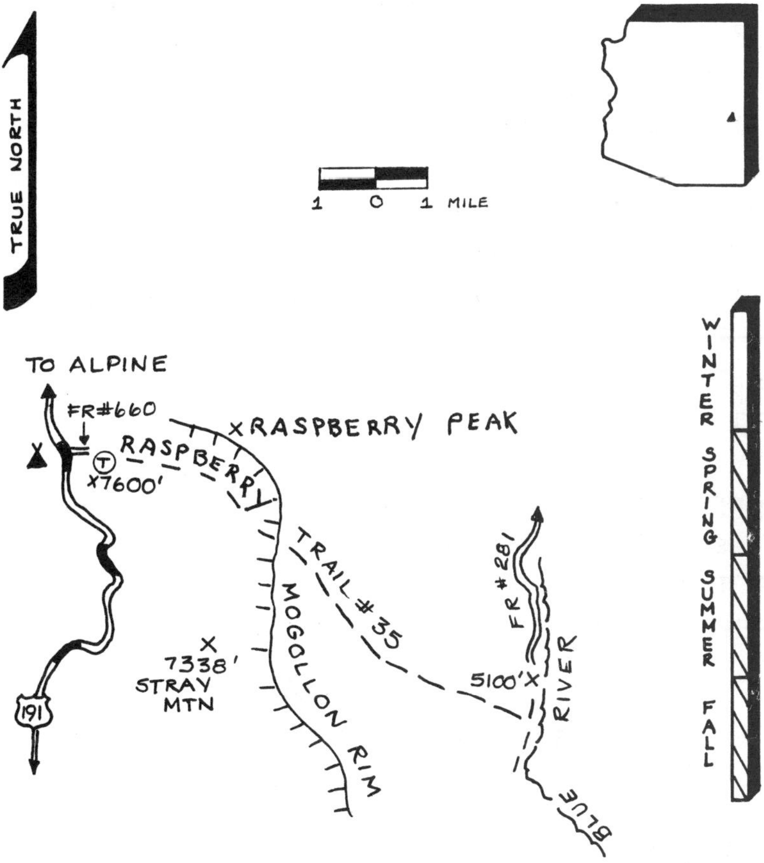

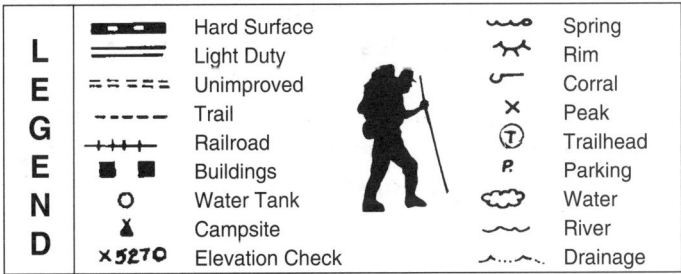

Hiking Central Arizona / 31

# STRAYHORSE CANYON TRAIL #20

**ATTRACTION:** Old fire cabin, running water at spring, scenery.

**REQUIREMENTS:** Food, water, sturdy boots, proper maps; car okay to trailhead; 5.5 hours hiking time one way.

**LOCATION:** Clifton Ranger District - Blue Ridge Wilderness.

**DIFFICULTY:** Difficult

**ELEVATIONS:** 8200' - 5000'

**LENGTH:** 12.7 miles one way

**MAPS REQUIRED:** U.S.G.S. 7.5 min. topographic for Rose Peak.

**PERMIT:** No

**BIKES:** No

**EQUESTRIAN:** Yes

**WATER:** Yes - purify

**INFORMATION:** Access to several other trails; study maps for car shuttle to avoid hike back up.

**FIREARMS:** Yes

**PETS ON LEASH:** Yes - leash or controlled

## TRAIL INFORMATION

Trailhead is at the Rose Peak turnoff 22 miles north of Granville on U.S. Route 191, by the picnic table.

The first 1.1 miles of this trail drops 800 feet into the canyon where an old fire cabin will be found. At 1.4 miles you will encounter a spring that runs all year. Following gentle slopes and nice stands of trees, while watching for views of Rose Peak fire tower. You will soon junction with Hagan Trail #31 at 6.6 miles, and Lengthy Trail #89 at 7.6 miles. At 8.8 miles a cabin and corral will be encountered. You will leave the canyon bottom at 9 miles for about 1/2 mile. At 12.7 miles, and the end of the trail, is its junction with the Blue River and Blue River Trail #101. This is about 1 mile below the end of the Blue River Road where a car could be parked.

# STRAYHORSE CANYON TRAIL #20

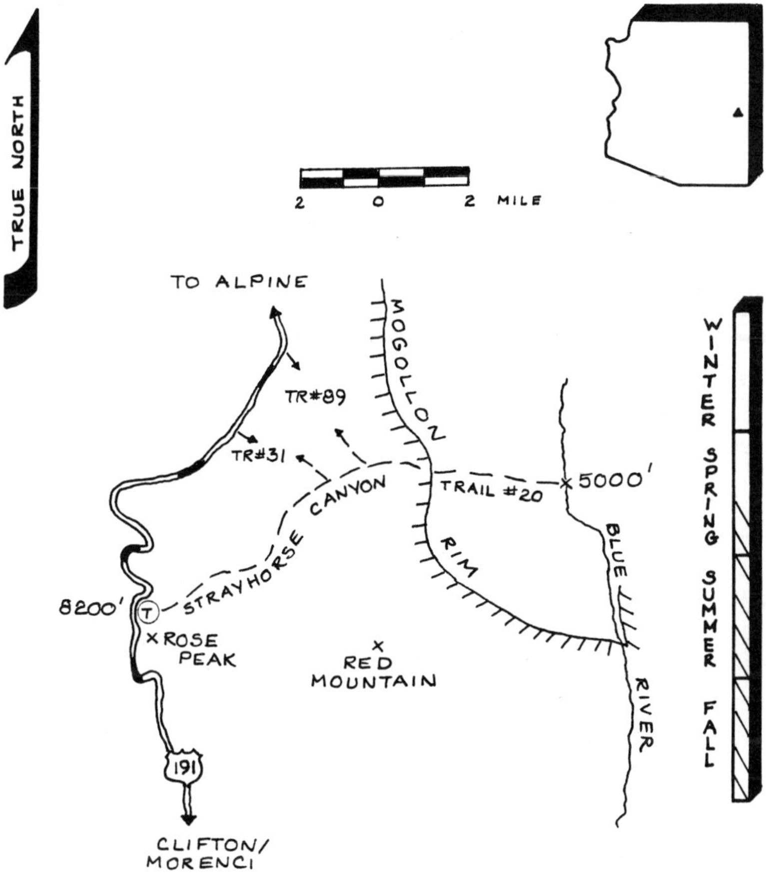

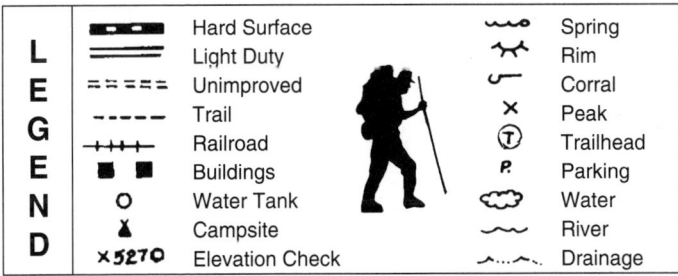

Hiking Central Arizona / 33

# ICEHOUSE CANYON TRAIL #198

**ATTRACTION:** Very nice views.

**REQUIREMENTS:** Food, water, sturdy boots, proper maps; car okay to trailhead; 8-9 hours hiking time round trip.

**LOCATION:** Globe Ranger District - Pinal Mountains.

**DIFFICULTY:** Difficult

**ELEVATIONS:** 3800' - 7520'

**LENGTH:** 9 miles round trip

**MAPS REQUIRED:** U.S.G.S. 7.5 min. topographic for Pinal Peak.

**PERMIT:** No

**BIKES:** Not recommended.

**EQUESTRIAN:** Yes    **WATER:** Yes. Best to bring your own.

**INFORMATION:** Can be very hot in summer as well as cold in the higher elevations. This hike is not for a novice.

**FIREARMS:** Yes    **PETS ON LEASH:** Yes

## TRAIL INFORMATION

To reach the trailhead, follow Jess Hayes Road southeast of Globe to the junction of Icehouse Canyon Road #112 and Sixshooter Canyon Road #222, and continue on Road 112. At the junction of Kellner Canyon Road #55 and Icehouse Canyon Road #112, at 2.4 miles, again continue on Road 112. Soon pavement will end. At about 4.5 miles will be the junction of Roads #112 and #112C; continue on 112 to 4.7 miles and the trailhead on the right side. Parking is past the trailhead.

Trail follows a jeep road along a ridge with a creek on your left. At 1.3 miles is a water tank and the junction of Kellner Canyon Trail #242 from the west joining Icehouse Canyon Trail. Continue on Icehouse Canyon Trail for 1 more mile to Dog House Spring. In .2 mile more is the junction of Telephone Trail coming from Sixshooter Canyon. Continue to the right through some switchbacks, and in 0.1 mile is another junction of sorts. Trail to the right goes to a spring; continue to the left. At 4.3 miles are some more switchbacks and then the end of the trail at Forest Road #651.

This could be a loop hike via Telephone Trail and Sixshooter Canyon Trail with a car shuttle.

# ICEHOUSE CANYON
# TRAIL #198

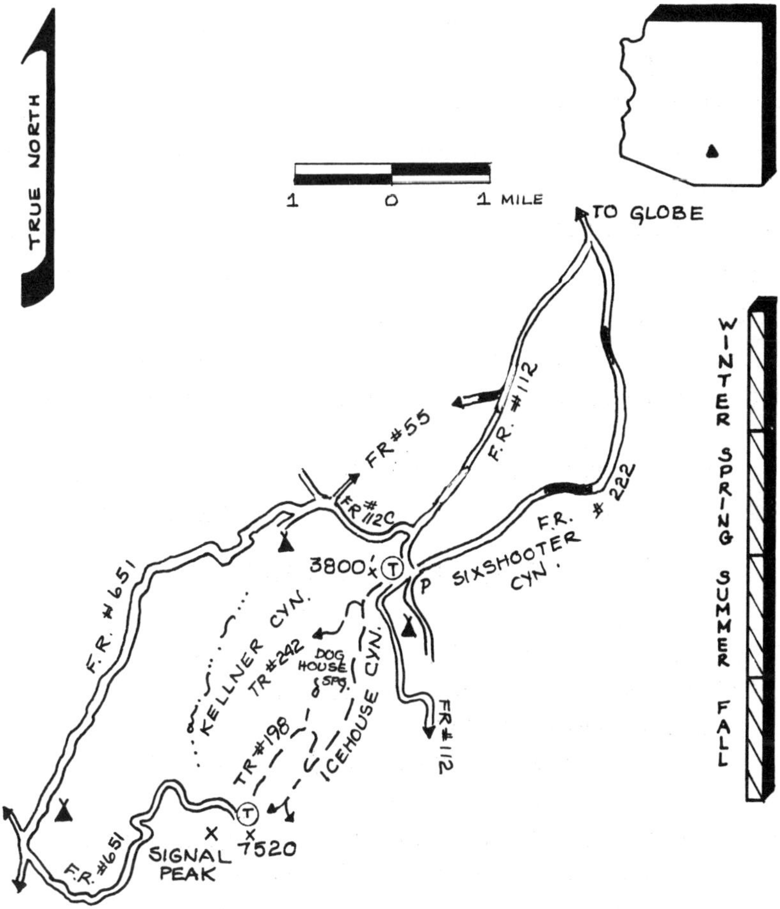

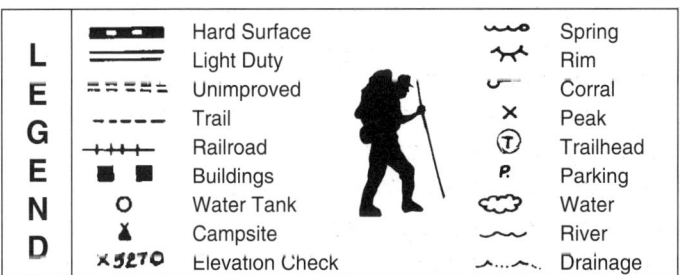

| LEGEND | | | | |
|---|---|---|---|---|
| ▬▬▬ | Hard Surface | ᗢᗢ | Spring |
| ═══ | Light Duty | ⌢⌢ | Rim |
| ═ ═ ═ | Unimproved | ⌒ | Corral |
| ─ ─ ─ | Trail | × | Peak |
| ┼┼┼┼ | Railroad | Ⓣ | Trailhead |
| ■ ■ | Buildings | P. | Parking |
| O | Water Tank | ᗣᗣ | Water |
| ▲ | Campsite | ⌒⌒ | River |
| ×5270 | Elevation Check | ⌒⌒⌒ | Drainage |

Hiking Central Arizona / 35

# KELLNER CANYON TRAIL #242

**ATTRACTION:** Extremely scenic and good test of one's skills.
**REQUIREMENTS:** Food, water, sturdy boots, proper maps; car okay to trailhead; 4 hours hiking time one way.
**LOCATION:** Globe Ranger District - Pinal Mountains.
**DIFFICULTY:** Difficult
**ELEVATIONS:** 7160' - 5200'
**LENGTH:** 4.1 miles one way to junction on Icehouse Canyon Trail #198.
**MAPS REQUIRED:** U.S.G.S. 7.5 min. topographic for Pinal Peak.
**PERMIT:** No           **BIKES:** Not recommended.
**EQUESTRIAN:** Yes, but rocky and dangerous.
**WATER:** Not dependable - best to bring your own.
**INFORMATION:** Trail is very rocky and hot. Be aware of possible flash flooding. Hike back up can be avoided via Icehouse Canyon Trail #198 and car shuttle.
**FIREARMS:** Yes           **PETS ON LEASH:** Yes

## TRAIL INFORMATION

Follow directions to trailhead for Sixshooter Canyon Trail. Stay on Icehouse Canyon Road #112 for 2.4 miles to the junction of Kellner Canyon Road #55 and take 55 to the right. Remain on 55 for 5.4 miles to junction with 651. Turn left and remain on 651 for 14 miles and park at trailhead just past a cattle guard.

Descend along a wash and through a narrow canyon, as you continue down past Kellner Canyon Spring and a gate you must open and close at .5 mile. Along with some ruins at 1.1 mile is a burn area with good views. You will have passed through another open/close gate. Trail continues northeast. In .1 mile trail will head east into another canyon. You will cross a wash and turn north. In .5 mile trail turns back to the south across a dry wash and then north again. There are nice views of the valley here. Trail will head northeast in about .8 mile as you cross a wash and leave the pines. Trail ends on Icehouse Canyon Trail #198.

Follow Icehouse Canyon Trail #198 to its lower trailhead. I have used this return for your total hiking time. Use a car shuttle.

# KELLNER CANYON TRAIL #242

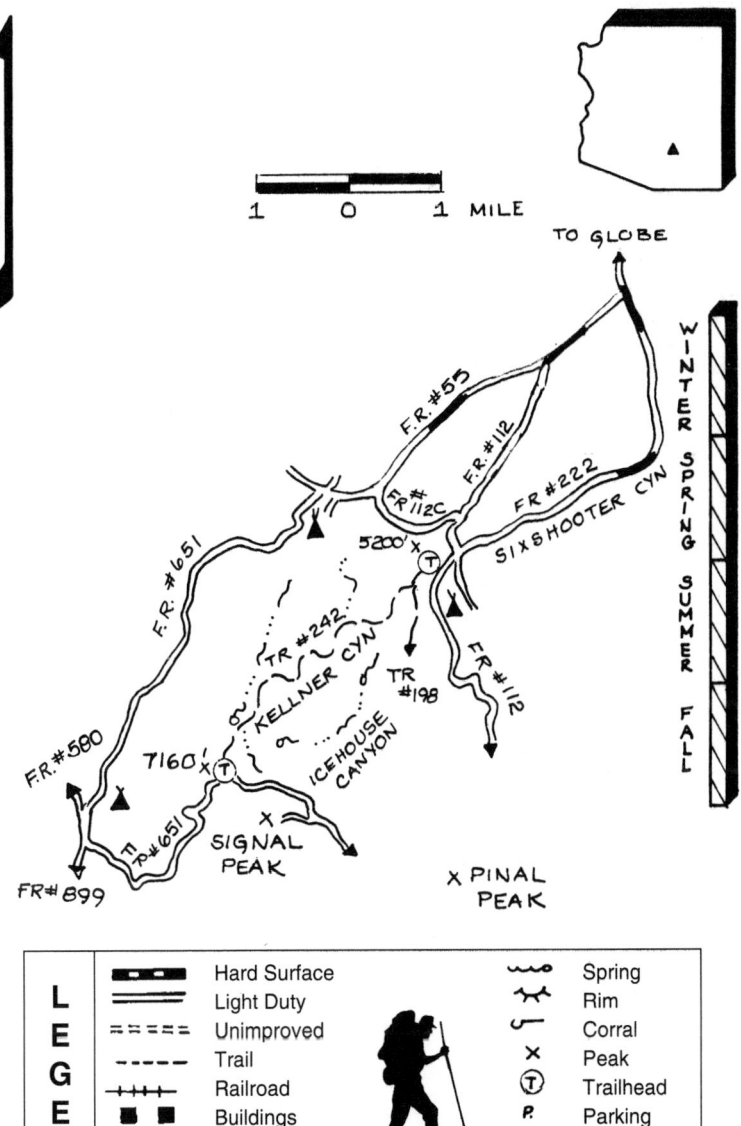

Hiking Central Arizona / 37

# SIXSHOOTER CANYON TRAIL #197

**ATTRACTION:** Good hike for beginning backpackers, nice scenery, good views.

**REQUIREMENTS:** Food, water, sturdy boots, proper maps; car okay to trailhead; 6-7 hours hiking time round trip.

**LOCATION:** Globe Ranger District - Pinal Mountains.

**DIFFICULTY:** Moderate

**ELEVATIONS:** 3800' - 7560'

**LENGTH:** 4.7 miles one way

**MAPS REQUIRED:** U.S.G.S. 7.5 min. topographic for Pinal Peak.

**PERMIT:** No     **BIKES:** No     **EQUESTRIAN:** Yes

**WATER:** Not dependable - bring your own.

**INFORMATION:** Hike can be very hot in summer as well as cold in the higher elevations.

**FIREARMS:** Yes     **PETS ON LEASH:** Yes

## TRAIL INFORMATION

To reach the trailhead, follow Jess Hayes Road southeast of Globe to the junction of Icehouse Canyon Road #112 and Sixshooter Canyon Road #222 (4.7 miles). Continue on Road 112 to parking area just before the bridge at Mile Post 6.3. Walk to the trailhead which will be on the right side of the road.

Trail travels southwest off Forest Road #112 on a jeep trail. At .4 mile a series of switchbacks are encountered as you follow and cross a creek many times on the trail. At .8 mile you will come to a fork. As you take the right fork, the trail becomes steeper, with nice views of the Globe/Miami area. At 3.5 miles the trail widens to 15 feet and is thickly wooded. Just before another fork, you will pass a mine on your left and the ruins of an old cabin.

The right fork is Telephone Trail that continues over to Icehouse Canyon Trail #198. Take the left fork and continue for about .5 mile to another fork, where you will turn right to the end of the trail at Ferndell Spring. This could be a loop hike via Telephone Trail and Icehouse Canyon Trail with a car shuttle.

# SIXSHOOTER CANYON TRAIL #197

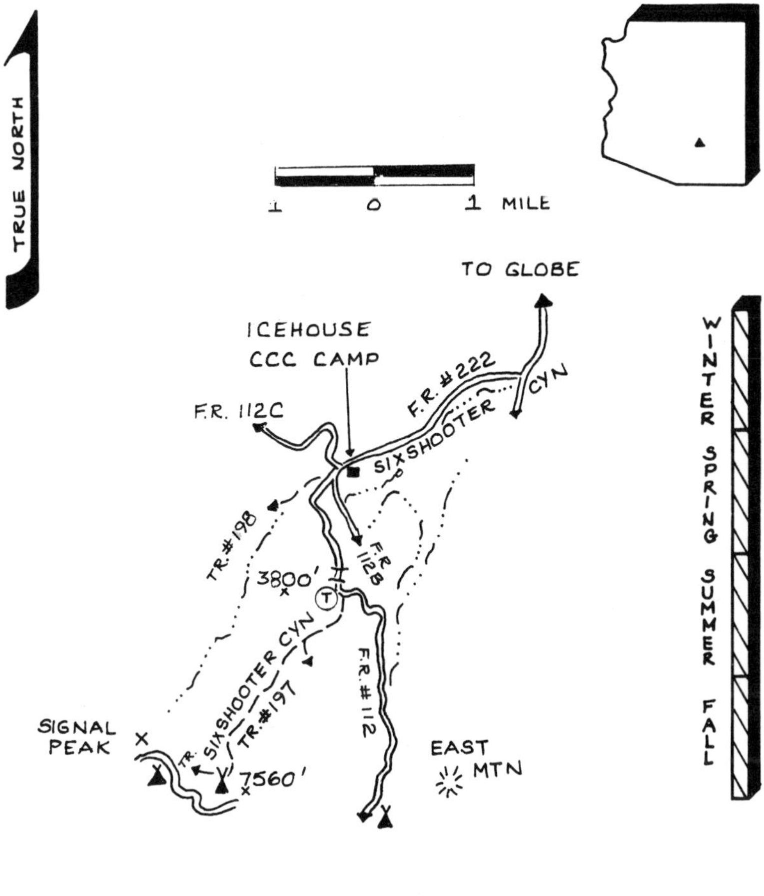

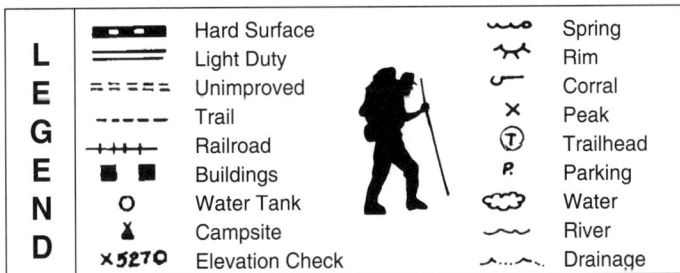

Hiking Central Arizona / 39

# SQUAW SPRING TRAIL #196

**ATTRACTION:** A variety of vegetation, very impressive view of Pioneer Basin at end of trail.

**REQUIREMENTS:** Food, water, sturdy boots, proper maps; car okay to trailhead; 3.5 hours hiking time round trip.

**LOCATION:** Globe Ranger District - Pinal Mountains.

**DIFFICULTY:** Moderate

**ELEVATIONS:** 7680' - 6156'

**LENGTH:** 2.1 miles one way

**MAPS REQUIRED:** U.S.G.S. 7.5 min. topographic for Pinal Peak.

**PERMIT:** No

**BIKES:** No

**EQUESTRIAN:** Yes

**WATER:** Not dependable - bring your own.

**INFORMATION:** Dress for thick ground cover. Area is open range.

**FIREARMS:** Yes        **PETS ON LEASH:** Yes

## TRAIL INFORMATION

Refer to trailhead information for Kellner Canyon Trail #242. At the 14-mile mark, continue on Road #651 to its junction with #651C, taking the right fork past twelve summer cabins. At 17.7 miles is the upper junction of 651 and 651C. The left fork goes to upper Pinal Campground. Follow the right fork to the trailhead. In .2 mile more is another fork where you will turn right. At 18 miles is a three-way fork where two roads turn right and the other goes straight ahead to a gravel pit. The trailhead is at the head of a drainage at the junction of #651D and one that runs around the base of the hill.

Trail follows in a drainage in a southeast direction and passes through an open/close gate at about .2 mile. Just past this gate, about .1 mile, is Squaw Spring.

In just over one more mile is a view of Pioneer Basin worth a lot of picture taking. Now, on a wide jeep trail, you will come to the end of the trail at Pioneer Pass trailhead. Return the same way.

# SQUAW SPRING TRAIL #196

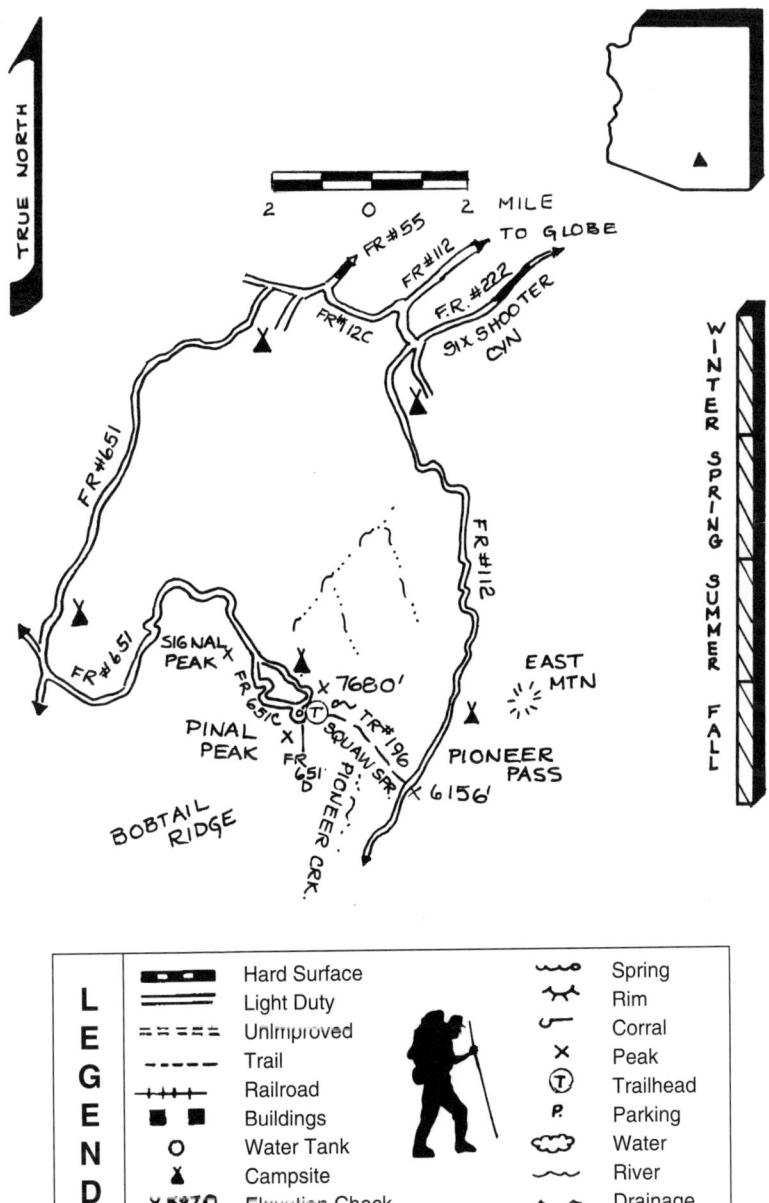

Hiking Central Arizona / 41

# TELEPHONE TRAIL #192

**ATTRACTION:** A possible loop hike between Sixshooter Canyon Trail and Icehouse Canyon Trail, nice views.

**REQUIREMENTS:** Food, water, sturdy boots, proper maps; trailhead access from Sixshooter Canyon Trail or Icehouse Canyon Trail; 1 hour hiking time one way.

**LOCATION:** Globe Ranger District - Pinal Mountains.

**DIFFICULTY:** Difficult

**ELEVATIONS:** 5960' - 6720'

**LENGTH:** 1.2 miles one way

**MAPS REQUIRED:** U.S.G.S. 7.5 min. topographic for Pinal Peak.

**PERMIT:** No

**BIKES:** No

**EQUESTRIAN:** Yes

**WATER:** No - bring your own.

**INFORMATION:** Very steep and rugged.

**FIREARMS:** Yes

**PETS ON LEASH:** Yes

## TRAIL INFORMATION

Follow directions for Sixshooter Canyon Trail #197 to a point 3.8 miles into the trail. Here is the start of Telephone Trail to its end on Icehouse Canyon Trail #198, at a point 2.5 miles from its lower trailhead.

At the creek near the ruins, on Sixshooter Canyon Trail #197, take the left fork past the cabin. At .7 mile turn right at the rock pile. A maintenance road travels north; be careful to follow the trail and not the road. At .9 mile you will begin your descent. The trail will terminate on Icehouse Canyon Trail #198 just .1 mile below Dog House Spring.

A car shuttle would work fine here if you returned to Icehouse Canyon's lower trailhead.

# TELEPHONE TRAIL #192

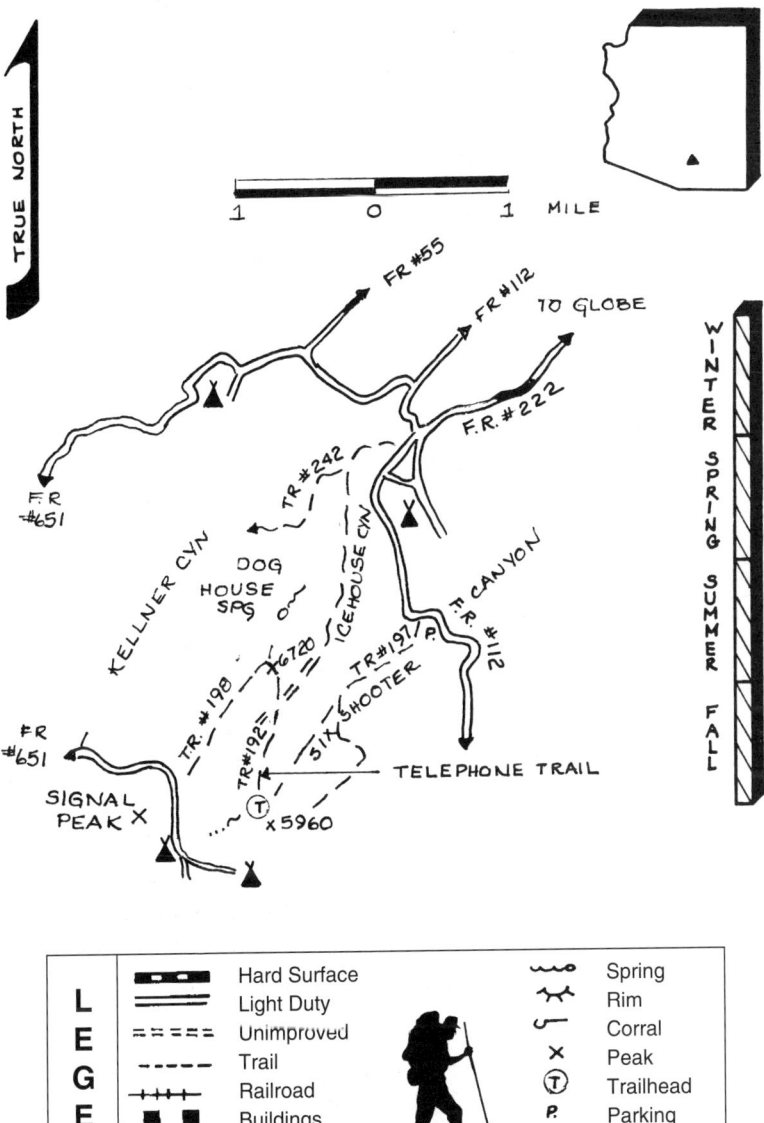

Hiking Central Arizona / 43

# AMETHYST TRAIL #253

**ATTRACTION:** Breathtaking views.

**REQUIREMENTS:** Food, water, sturdy boots, proper maps; car okay to trailhead of Four Peaks Trail; 2 hours hiking time round trip just on Amethyst Trail #253.

**LOCATION:** Mesa Ranger District - Four Peaks.

**DIFFICULTY:** Difficult

**ELEVATIONS:** 5800' - 6880'

**LENGTH:** 3 miles one way

**MAPS REQUIRED:** U.S.G.S. 7.5 min. topographic for Four Peaks.

**PERMIT:** No

**BIKES:** No

**EQUESTRIAN:** Not recommended.

**WATER:** No - bring your own.

**INFORMATION:** Access is from Four Peaks Trail; it is a moderate to difficult hike to get to Amethyst Trail trailhead. Contains a lot of brush.

**FIREARMS:** Yes

**PETS ON LEASH:** Yes

## TRAIL INFORMATION

Follow trailhead directions to Four Peaks Trail #130. Follow Four Peaks Trail Information to Amethyst Trail #253, which turns right off Four Peaks Trail in just over a mile, at a very evident saddle. It is not marked so you must pay close attention due to overgrowth.

From here the trail climbs steeply to Brown's Saddle before skirting the peaks. Trail terminates at an amethyst mine. Do not trespass; it is very private property. Return the same way.

# AMETHYST TRAIL #253

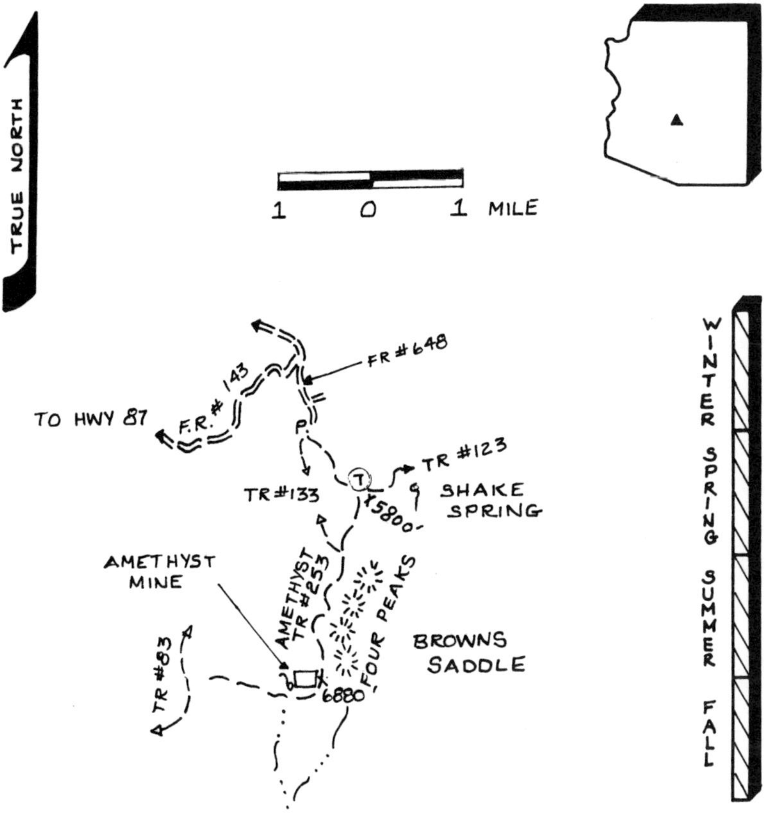

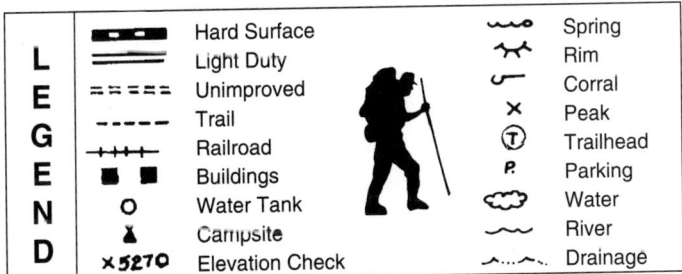

Hiking Central Arizona / 45

# BROWN'S TRAIL #133

**ATTRACTION:** Trail offers an easy route to the Amethyst Mine/ Brown's Saddle area.

**REQUIREMENTS:** Water, food, sturdy boots, proper maps; pickup truck best to trailhead; 1.5 hours hiking time one way.

**LOCATION:** Mesa Ranger District, northeast of Fountain Hills State Route 87.

**DIFFICULTY:** Moderate

**ELEVATIONS:** 5700' - 6800'

**LENGTH:** Approximately 2 miles one way.

**MAPS REQUIRED:** U.S.G.S. 7.5 min. topographic for Four Peaks.

**PERMIT:** No

**BIKES:** No

**EQUESTRIAN:** Yes

**WATER:** No - bring your own.

**INFORMATION:** Brown's Peak is extremely dangerous. Do not climb without someone knowing your destination.

**FIREARMS:** Yes

**PETS ON LEASH:** Yes

## TRAIL INFORMATION

Access to trailhead is by taking State Route 87 towards Payson. About 21 miles from Mesa, you will see a sign for Four Peaks Road; turn right. The road will "T" in about 19 miles, and another right turn and two more miles will bring you to the trailhead.

This trail begins at Lone Pine Saddle (BB) which is the trailhead for Brown's Trail as well as the Four Peaks Trail #130. The Brown's Trail heads south in a series of leisurely switchbacks leading steadily uphill toward Amethyst Trail #253.

This is the easiest and shortest route to the popular Brown's Peak. Trail #253 leads a short distance to Brown's Saddle where skilled climbers begin the ascent to Brown's Peak. There are no officially designated routes to the top of Brown's Peak and climbers are urged to exercise extreme caution making the ascent.

# BROWN'S TRAIL #133

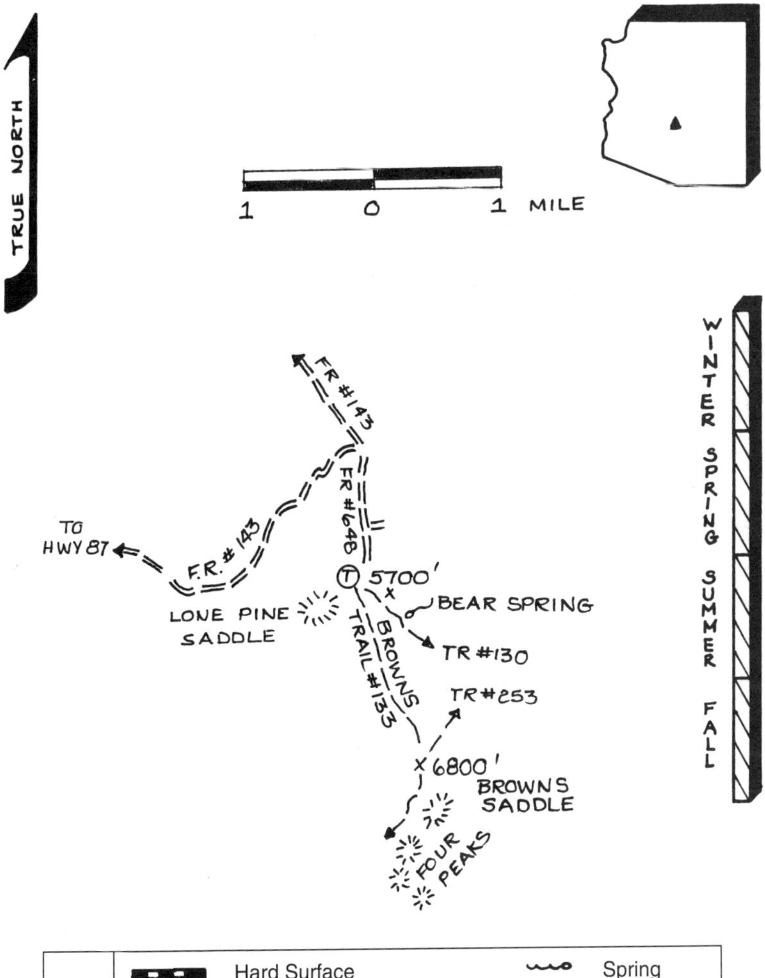

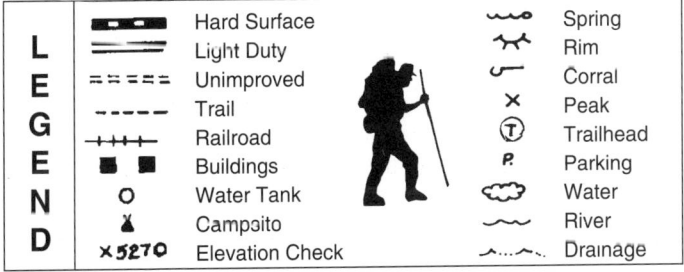

Hiking Central Arizona / 47

# FOUR PEAKS TRAIL #130

**ATTRACTION:** Excellent views of Tonto Basin and Four Peaks, excellent wooded sections, access to many other trails.

**REQUIREMENTS:** Lots of water and food, sturdy boots, proper maps; pickup truck best to trailhead; 6 hours hiking time one way.

**LOCATION:** Mesa Ranger District, northeast of Fountain Hills.

**DIFFICULTY:** Difficult

**ELEVATIONS:** 6200' - 3800'

**LENGTH:** Approximately 10.0 miles one way

**MAPS REQUIRED:** U.S.G.S. 7.5 min. topographic for Four Peaks - Theodore Roosevelt Dam.

**PERMIT:** No

**BIKES:** No

**EQUESTRIAN:** Yes

**WATER:** No - bring your own.

**INFORMATION:** Trail skirts the Four Peaks Mountain area and follows Buckhorn Ridge to Buckhorn Mountain, part of Arizona Trail. Trail not for a novice.

**FIREARMS:** Yes

**PETS ON LEASH:** Yes

## TRAIL INFORMATION

Access to trailhead is on State Rt. 87 towards Payson from Mesa. About 21 miles from Mesa is a sign for Four Peaks Rd. Turn right and the road will "T" in about 19 miles. Another right turn and 2 more miles will take you to the trailhead. This trail begins as an old jeep track (now closed to vehicles) at Lone Pine Saddle and contours for about 1 mile to the junction with Amethyst Trail. At this point the trail changes to a pack trail. Shortly thereafter, the trail descends about 300 feet to a drainage; Shake Springs is just beyond. Trail then contours over to the junction with Oak Flat Trail #123; turn right here. Now the trail climbs at a moderate gradient to an excellent viewpoint of Tonto Basin. It then contours around the rugged east side of Brown's Peak, reaching a high point just

(Continued on Page 50)

# FOUR PEAKS TRAIL #130

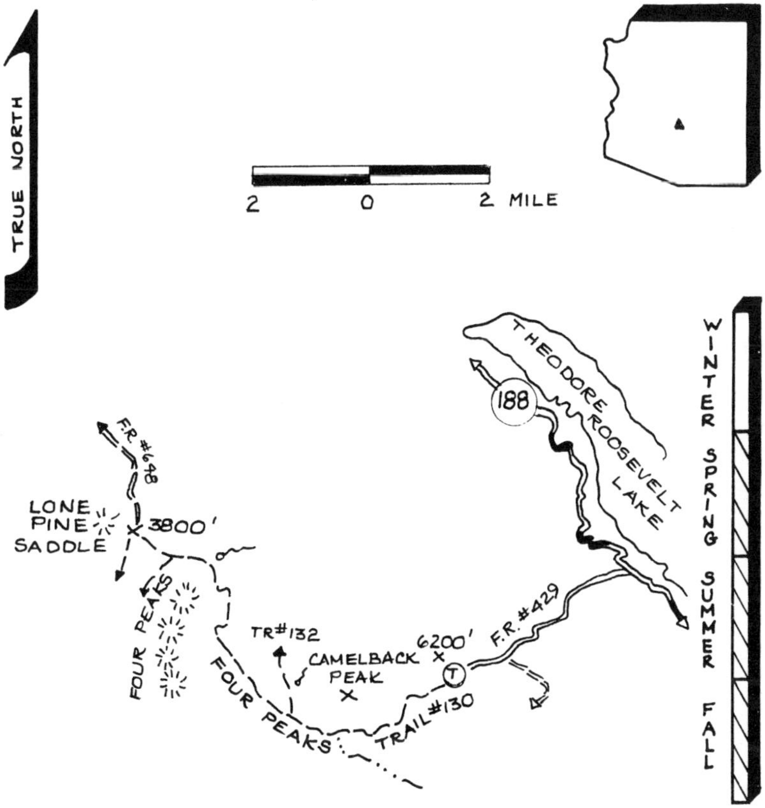

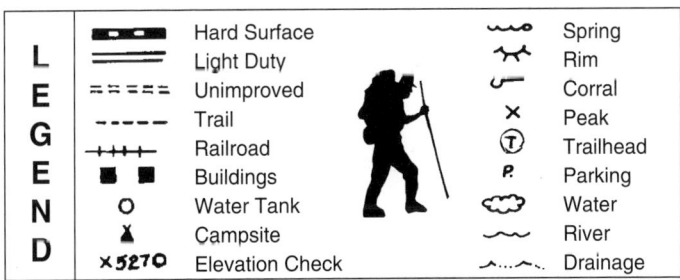

Hiking Central Arizona / 49

(Continued from Page 48)

before descending sharply into a prominent canyon. The junction with Alder Creek Trail is found just after crossing the drainage in this canyon. Four Peaks Trail turns left and contours, largely through dense chaparral, around to Black Bear Saddle, the lowest point between Buckhorn Mountain and Four Peaks. The trail then climbs steeply, following Buckhorn Ridge to the summit of Buckhorn Mountain. Parts of this section may be hard to follow. Chillicut Trail has its southern terminus just north of the summit of Buckhorn Mountain and the Four Peaks Trail continues just south of the summit. The summit itself is signed. From the summit of Buckhorn Mountain, the trail continues east to Granite Springs (cannot be counted on as a permanent source of water) which is reached after a one-mile steep descent; there is another short descent to Hackberry Creek. Trail then runs out a ridge to a high point before dropping by a series of well-defined switchbacks to Buckhorn Creek. After pulling out of Buckhorn Creek to another high point, the trail drops at a moderate rate for about 3/4 of a mile to meet Forest Road #429.

Four Peaks Trail #130 is not for the novice! Great views, though, and access to many other trails.
(Photo by John Villinski)

Giant saguaro beside the Peralta Trail.
(Photo by John Villinski)

Some trail signage may be a little hard to find!
(Photo by John Villinski)

Weaver's Needle—a well-known landmark!
(Photo by John Villinski)

# PERALTA TRAIL #102

**ATTRACTION:** Weaver's Needle, legendary home of the Lost Dutchman's gold.

**REQUIREMENTS:** Food, water, sturdy boots, proper maps; car okay to trailhead; 4-5 hours hiking time round trip.

**LOCATION:** Mesa Ranger District - Superstition Mountains.

**DIFFICULTY:** Moderate

**ELEVATIONS:** 2400' - 3760' - 3310'

**LENGTH:** 6.3 miles round trip

**MAPS REQUIRED:** U.S.G.S. 7.5 min. topographic for Weaver's Needle.

**PERMIT:** No

**BIKES:** No

**EQUESTRIAN:** Yes

**WATER:** No - bring your own.

**INFORMATION:** Canyon prone to treacherous flash flooding and severe storms; hot in summer.

**FIREARMS:** Yes

**PETS ON LEASH:** Yes

## TRAIL INFORMATION

Take Rt. 60/70 east from Apache Junction approximately 8 miles to the Peralta Road #77 turnoff. The trailhead is about 7.3 miles down this road, just past the Dons Camp at a large parking area.

As you start your hike, the canyon walls not only rise above you but close in on you as well. There are shady spots along the way to rest. You will see where much erosion has taken place on the canyon walls. At this point you are within 10 minutes of Freemont Saddle, and there Weaver's Needle will suddenly appear—good picture area.

Now descending, you will encounter a few switchbacks, and past the Needle it is only 1 mile to Pinyon Camp and the end of the trail. This is also a nice place to rest. Return the same way.

# PERALTA TRAIL #102

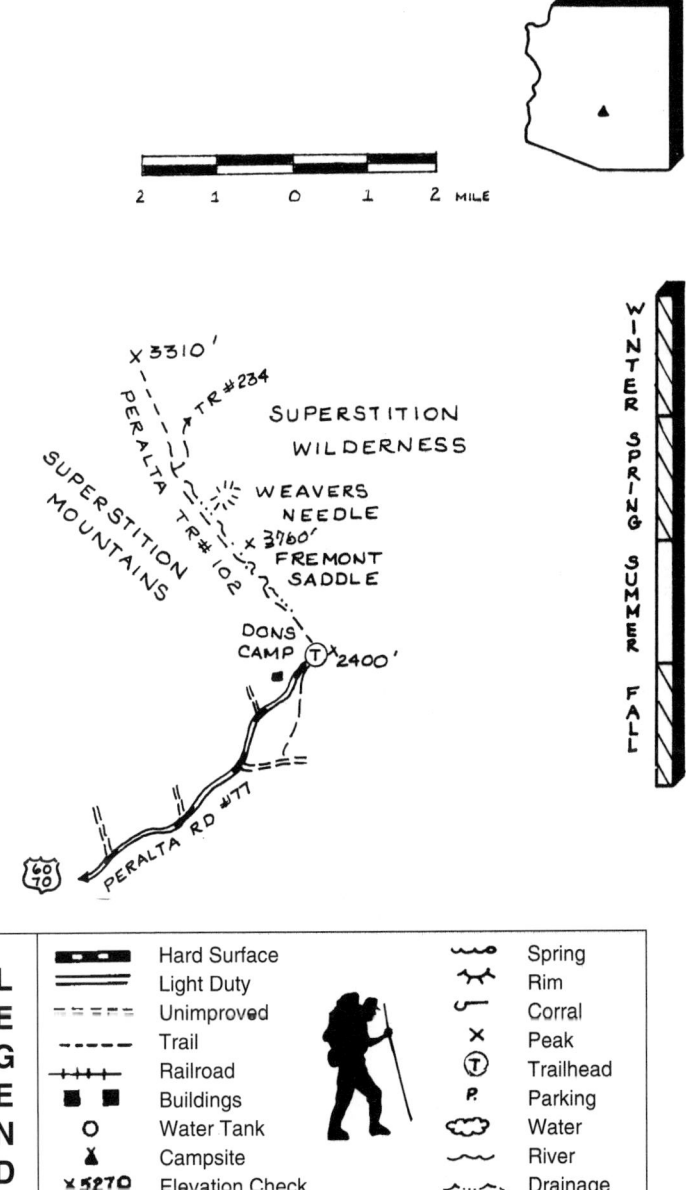

*Hiking Central Arizona* / 53

# PIGEON TRAIL #134

**ATTRACTION:** Nice hike for beginners, makes for a nice day along with the drive to the trailhead.

**REQUIREMENTS:** Food, water, sturdy boots, proper maps; car okay to trailhead; 2 hours hiking time round trip.

**LOCATION:** Mesa Ranger District - Four Peaks.

**DIFFICULTY:** Easy to Moderate.

**ELEVATIONS:** 5440' - 5640'

**LENGTH:** 2 miles one way

**MAPS REQUIRED:** U.S.G.S. 7.5 min. topographic for Four Peaks.

**PERMIT:** No

**BIKES:** No

**EQUESTRIAN:** Yes - rough road.

**WATER:** Not dependable - bring your own.

**INFORMATION:** Trail reconstructed and in good shape. This can be a nice loop hike via Four Peaks Trail #130.

**FIREARMS:** Yes

**PETS ON LEASH:** Yes

## TRAIL INFORMATION

Follow the trailhead directions for Four Peaks Trail #130 to Lone Pine Saddle. Just before Lone Pine Saddle there are a couple of parking spaces on your left. This is the Pigeon Trail #134 trailhead.

For the first 1/4 mile or so, this is a jeep road leading to Pigeon Spring. You will encounter a hairpin right turn at the spring. You will enjoy the rest of the trail as you hike through the always welcome ponderosa pine.

You can return by a right turn on Four Peaks Trail back to Lone Pine Saddle. Only a short walk from the saddle will take you back to your car.

# PIGEON TRAIL #134

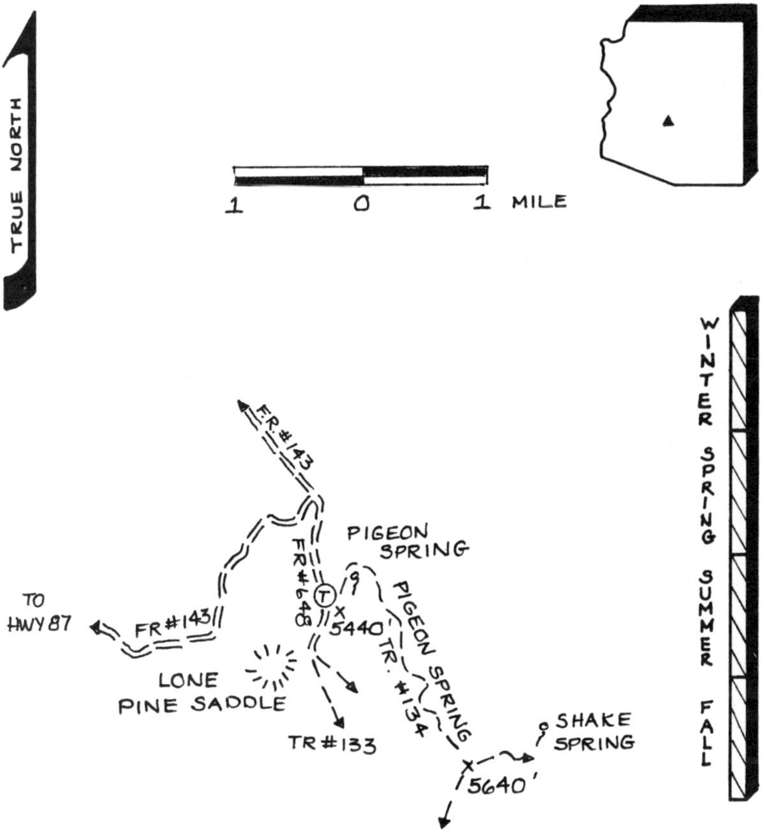

*Hiking Central Arizona* / 55

# BABE HAUGHT TRAIL #143

**ATTRACTION:** Fantastic views, remote location, historical trail.
**REQUIREMENTS:** Water, food, sturdy boots, proper maps; car okay to trailhead; 2.5 hours hiking time one way.
**LOCATION:** Payson Ranger District - fish hatchery to Rim Road.
**DIFFICULTY:** Moderate
**ELEVATIONS:** 6400' - 7700'
**LENGTH:** 2.2 miles one way
**MAPS REQUIRED:** U.S.G.S. 7.5 min. topographic for Knoll Lake.
**PERMIT:** No
**BIKES:** Yes          **EQUESTRIAN:** Yes
**WATER:** Not dependable - bring your own.
**INFORMATION:** Summer storms gather quickly here.
**FIREARMS:** Yes          **PETS ON LEASH:** Yes

## TRAIL INFORMATION

Take Highway 260 east out of Payson past Control Road to FR #289 and make a left turn here. This road takes you to the parking lot just outside the fish hatchery. You must hike through the fish hatchery property to gain access to the trailhead that is in back of the far buildings. It is best to let the Ranger District personnel know your plans while on hatchery property. Check for proper signs on a 4x4 post.

Trail starts by left turn out of hatchery area, followed by an abrupt uphill climb. Trail has a lot of uphill climbs, getting heavy about the .7 mile mark and continuing to the top. You will encounter a false crest of the rim to be followed by the true crest shortly. Some areas are rocky but passable, and very shady. You will know when you have reached the true top when you see a tree notched with a "T" facing downhill travelers. Great care must be taken from this point in following the remainder of trail to the trailhead at FR #300. Very few markings are found and only a few cairns. Trail will intersect with Forest Road #300, 27 miles northwest of Hwy. 260.

The Babe Haught Trail was built by Anderson Lee "Babe" Haught and his brother to pack crops and supplies to Winslow. This area is very primitive and has fantastic views. It is unique.

# BABE HAUGHT TRAIL #143

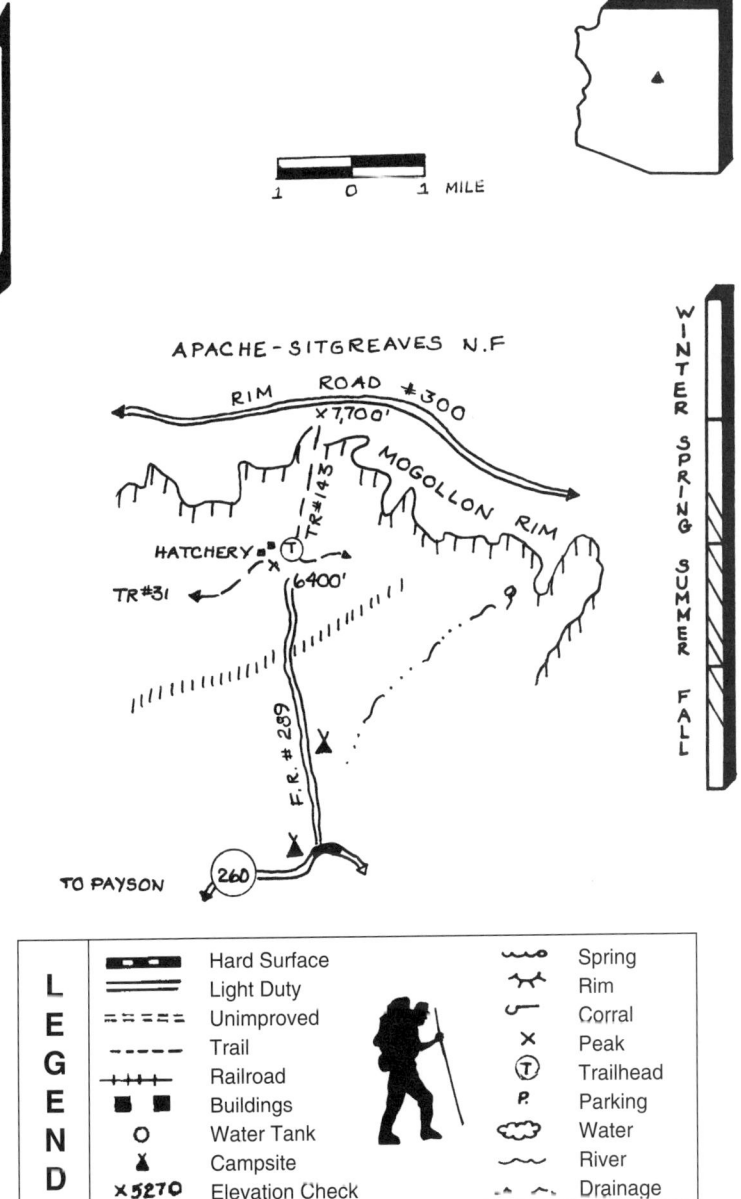

| LEGEND | | | | |
|---|---|---|---|---|
| ▬▬ | Hard Surface | | ᴗᴗᴗ | Spring |
| ▬▬▬ | Light Duty | | ≈ | Rim |
| ═ ═ ═ | Unimproved | | ⌒ | Corral |
| - - - - | Trail | | × | Peak |
| +++ | Railroad | | Ⓣ | Trailhead |
| ■ ■ | Buildings | | P. | Parking |
| O | Water Tank | | ☁ | Water |
| ⚑ | Campsite | | ~~ | River |
| ×5270 | Elevation Check | | ⸱⌒⸱⌒ | Drainage |

Hiking Central Arizona / 57

# HIGHLINE TRAIL #31

**ATTRACTION:** This trail takes you back in time and gives you a feeling of what the settlers went through long ago. Unmatched scenery!

**REQUIREMENTS:** Water, food, sturdy boots, proper maps; car okay to trailhead; 4-5 days hiking time one way.

**LOCATION:** Tonto National Forest-Payson Ranger District. Pine trailhead on Rt. 87 to Rt. 260; trailhead N.E. of Payson.

**DIFFICULTY:** Moderate to Difficult (because of length).

**ELEVATIONS:** 5380' - 7500' - 6900'

**LENGTH:** 51 miles one way.

**MAPS REQUIRED:** Quadrangles - 7.5 minute series topographic as follows:

1. Pine, Gila County
2. Buckhead Mesa
3. Kehl Ridge
4. Dane Canyon
5. Diamond Point
6. Promontory Butte
7. Knoll Lake
8. Promontory Butte (2nd time)
9. Woods Canyon

Maps 1 & 9 are the trailhead maps. The Highline Trail is not on either map but is very easy to follow. This is explained in detail under Trail Information.

**PERMIT:** No

**BIKES:** Yes - non-motorized.

**EQUESTRIAN:** Yes

**WATER:** Yes, as listed below, but TREAT ALL WATER!

Red Rock Spring, Pine Spring, Webber Creek, Bray Creek, Chase Creek, East Verde River, Dude Creek, Bonita Creek, Perley Creek, Ellison Creek, Tonto Creek, Dick Williams Creek, Horton Spring, Christopher Creek.

**INFORMATION:** Severe thunder and lightning storms can develop during July and August. Plan this hike giving careful consideration to the weather. Make sure your backpack and contents are complete.

(Continued on Page 60)

# HIGHLINE TRAIL #31

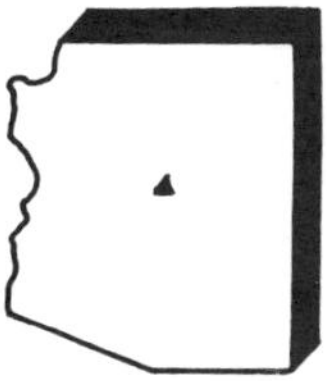

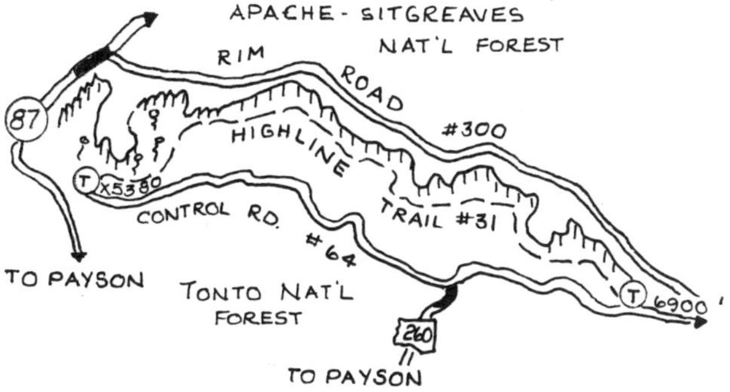

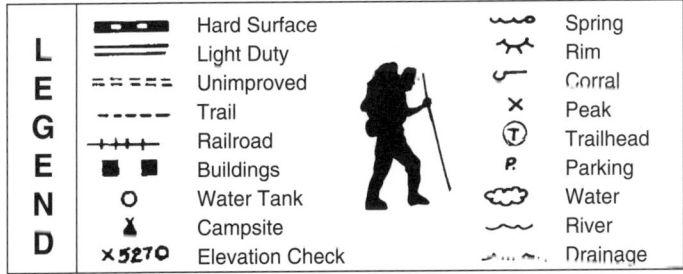

| | | Hard Surface | | Spring |
|---|---|---|---|---|
| L | | Light Duty | | Rim |
| E | = = = = | Unimproved | | Corral |
| G | - - - - - | Trail | × | Peak |
| E | +++++ | Railroad | Ⓣ | Trailhead |
| N | ■ ■ | Buildings | P. | Parking |
| D | O | Water Tank | | Water |
| | ⏚ | Campsite | | River |
| | ×5270 | Elevation Check | | Drainage |

Hiking Central Arizona / 59

The 1990 Dude Fire burned over 20 miles of this area; the trail is still open but it would be best to stay on the trail throughout this area as dangers still exist. Do not hike the trail unless someone knows your plans.

**FIREARMS:** Yes

**PETS ON LEASH:** Yes

## TRAIL INFORMATION

Pine trailhead is reached by going 15 miles north of Payson and is located just off Highway 87 on Forest Road 297. The 260 trailhead is located 27 miles east of Payson just off Highway 260. Facilities at both trailheads include a toilet, corral and large parking areas.

This trail is in the area known as the Rim Country that is just short of 8000 feet in altitude. This area is bordered by the east-to-west Control Road on the bottom and Forest Road #300 (Rim Road) on the top, with literally miles of room for the Highline Trail in between.

I am only sorry that there is not enough room available in this book for a more detailed description of this trail. You will be very taken in by its MANY rewards along the way; however, to hike this trail, you will have to work very hard, both physically and mentally. If you are not a veteran hiker, do not attempt this trail by yourself, and always advise someone of your plans, veteran or not.

Be aware and prepared for the fact that, due to the thoughtlessness of others, signs and cairns put there by the Forest Service to help you find your way will not always be in place. You will probably have to work at finding your way in many areas.

Besides becoming very familiar with all maps involved with the Highline Trail, and knowing your physical limitations, I make this suggestion. My first book, **Hiking Arizona,** is a must to have along on this hike, as it contains all trails from the Highline to the top of the Rim, as well as from the Highline down to the Control Road. It includes 18 trails that spur off the Highline, along with all needed information making possible any challenge you care to put together. You could spend all summer in this area. These trails cover about 120 miles. I wish I had time to go along.

*Apache pines along the Highline Trail.*

# HORTON CREEK TRAIL #285

**ATTRACTION:** A relaxing hike with the sound of water flowing for most of the trail.

**REQUIREMENTS:** Water, snack, sturdy boots, proper maps; car okay to trailhead; 2 hours hiking time one way.

**LOCATION:** Payson Ranger District - Horton Campground north to intersection with Highline Trail.

**DIFFICULTY:** Easy

**ELEVATIONS:** 5500' - 6420'

**LENGTH:** 3.8 miles one way.

**MAPS REQUIRED:** U.S.G.S. 7.5 min. topographic for Promontory Butte.

**PERMIT:** No

**BIKES:** Yes

**EQUESTRIAN:** Yes

**WATER:** Yes - unless weather has been extremely dry.

**INFORMATION:** Summer storms gather quickly here; ideal camping areas.

**FIREARMS:** Yes

**PETS ON LEASH:** Yes

## TRAIL INFORMATION

Trailhead is in upper corner of campground at intersection of Horton Creek and Forest Road #289. A sign is in place that directs you downhill through a dry wash and up the other side. Hiking now on left side of wash, a cattle gate is encountered at .25 mile. At .70 mile, the trail leaves the wash for a short distance and starts gently uphill. You will find very few markings, but you will almost always be within sound of Horton Creek. Trail follows old logging road most of the time. Area is open and easy hiking.

At 2.70 miles, the trail continues through two 20-foot logs laid on the ground and then turns sharply left. A fork in the trail is encountered at the 3-mile mark. Continuing on the right fork along the creek, many small waterfalls are encountered as well as an

(Continued on Page 64)

# HORTON CREEK TRAIL #285

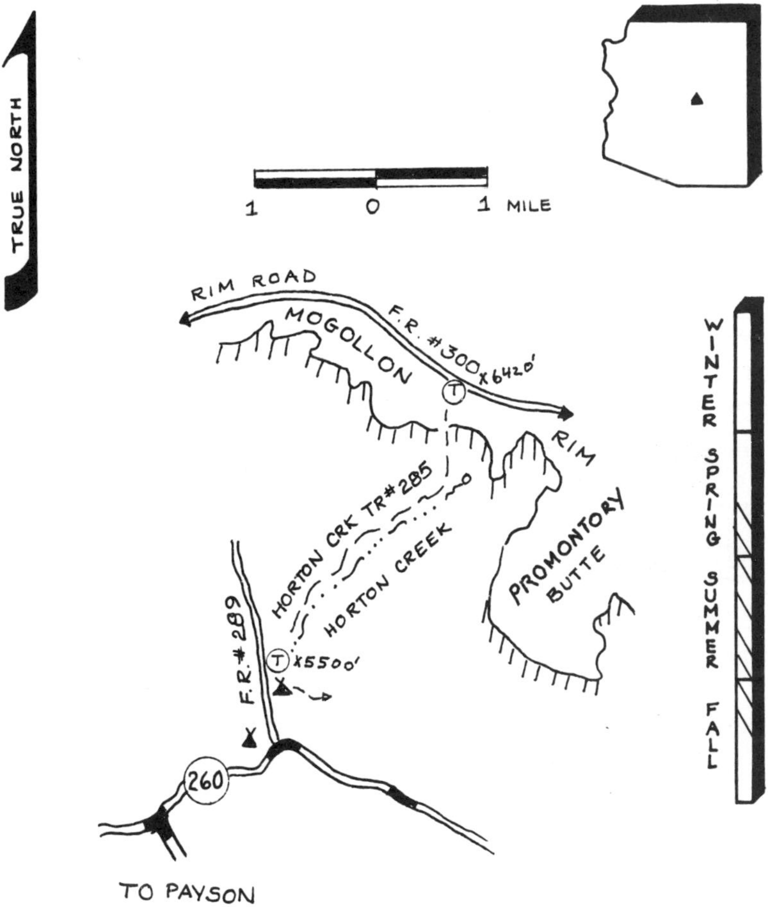

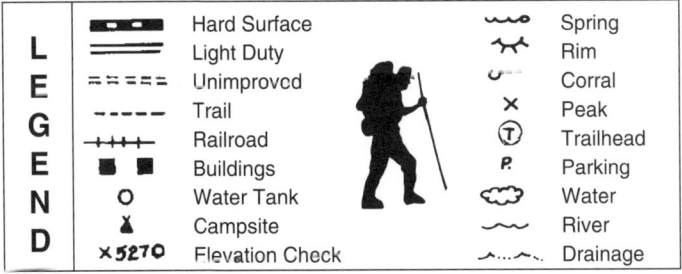

*Hiking Central Arizona* / 63

(Continued from Page 62)

alligator juniper with a 19-foot circumference. This is truly a relaxing area to be enjoyed.

Shortly after, more rocks are encountered, as well as a few switchbacks. At 3.85 miles, you will intersect with Highline Trail #31 at Horton Spring. This spring always flows generously.

Traveling straight from this intersection will take you to the top of the Rim via Horton Spring Trail #292. A left turn on Highline Trail #31 takes you to Tonto Creek just below the fish hatchery, and a right turn takes you to Promontory Butte Trail #278, as well as Derrick Trail #33. This is a rewarding hike with many possibilities.

This trail provides good opportunities for short, day hikes from Horton Campground or, in combination with lower Derrick, makes a good all-day hike.

Horton Spring is an unusually large spring, a popular camping area on Highline Trail. Trout fishing is good along Horton Creek.

Horton Spring Trail #292 from here to top of Rim is very steep. It was used by Zane Grey and Babe Haught to reach hunting area above Rim.

*One of Mother Nature's smallest creatures, a wood borer, creates a beautiful design for your viewing pleasure!*
*(Photo by John Villinski)*

*Beautiful Horton Creek.
(Photo by John Villinski)*

# PINE CANYON TRAIL #26

**ATTRACTION:** Fantastic views of Rim country, huge ponderosa pines.

**REQUIREMENTS:** Lots of water, food, sturdy boots, proper maps; car okay to trailhead; 6 hours hiking time one way.

**LOCATION:** Payson Ranger District, northeast of Pine.

**DIFFICULTY:** Moderate

**ELEVATIONS:** 7250' - 5380'

**LENGTH:** 7.2 miles one way.

**MAPS REQUIRED:** U.S.G.S. 7.5 min. topographic for Pine.

**PERMIT:** No

**BIKES:** Yes

**EQUESTRIAN:** Yes

**WATER:** Not dependable - bring your own.

**INFORMATION:** Storms gather quickly here; know how to find your way before attempting this trail.

**FIREARMS:** Yes

**PETS ON LEASH:** Yes

## TRAIL INFORMATION

This is the longest access trail from the north to Pine Trailhead. It is for hikers who love a physical challenge to test their abilities to find their way in some poorly marked areas. It's no place for a novice to go it alone.

As it is a very long hike, I would suggest using two cars. This hike can be made in a day, but do start early.

On Rt. 87, continue driving on through Payson until you reach the Pine Trailhead, just south of Pine (well marked). Leaving one car at this location, drive on through Pine on Rt. 87 until mile marker 279.1. Park here and, after you go through the gate, you are at the start of Pine Canyon Trail.

It is imperative that you diligently watch for double-notch markings on the trees to guide you. Concentrate on the markings for the entire length, as many trails branch off along the way.

(Continued on Page 68)

# PINE CANYON TRAIL #26

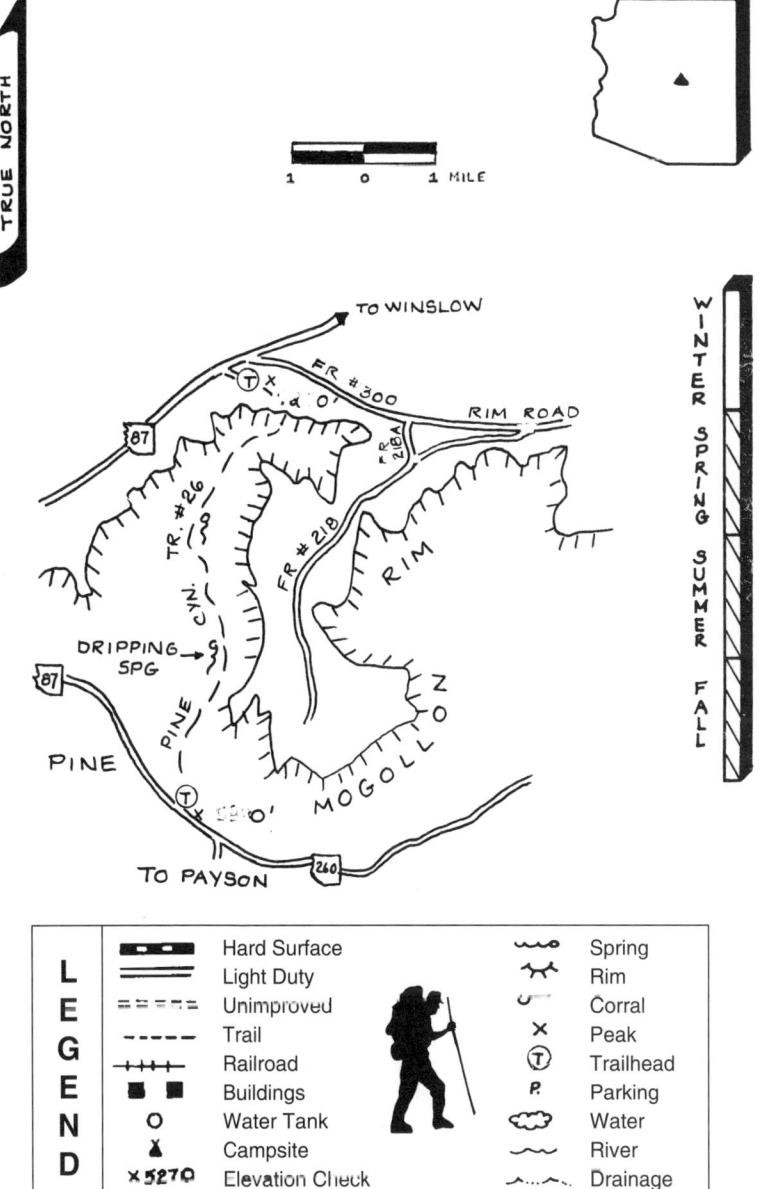

| LEGEND | | | | |
|---|---|---|---|---|
| | Hard Surface | | ⌣⌣o | Spring |
| | Light Duty | | ⋏⋏⋏ | Rim |
| | Unimproved | | ⌣ | Corral |
| | Trail | | × | Peak |
| +++ | Railroad | | Ⓣ | Trailhead |
| ■ ■ | Buildings | | P. | Parking |
| O | Water Tank | | ⌢⌣ | Water |
| ⚐ | Campsite | | ~~ | River |
| ×527○ | Elevation Check | | ⌁...⌁ | Drainage |

Hiking Central Arizona / 67

(Continued from Page 66)

Remember, this is Trail #26.

At the start of the trail is a fence on the left. Do not, at any time, cross through it, even though it may seem the way to go. You will come to a gate in the fence at about .2 mile; do not enter, continue straight.

Soon, stone cairns will appear on the right and the trail gets easier to follow. At .3 mile will be a cairn on the left marking the direct descent, via switchbacks, into Schall Canyon. Be prepared to take in a fantastic view, as you are about to be enveloped in 100 square miles of nature, so don't forget your camera. Even though these switchbacks are in good shape, there will still be a sense of adventure as you descend very quickly. Along with the many pines are alligator junipers, yuccas and sizable manzanita.

At the creek bottom, signs point to places such as "Spradling Canyon", "Cinch Hook Butte", "The Deep Pools" and "Waterfall". They are good reference points, but don't stray from the trail.

A few miles past the creek is a lovely meadow at "Parsnip Springs". The spring is flowing about two feet wide along the left side of the trail. The trail here turns into a road, and the black and yellow signs indicate this is a study area.

Watch on the left for a sign that says, "Dripping Springs" and "Highline Trail". *Make a 90-degree left turn. Continuing straight instead is forbidden, as it is 100% private property.*

After the left turn, the trail will ascend and become more rugged. You will have to become alert now for tree markings. In about a half mile or so, after excellent views of Pine, you will arrive at "Dripping Springs". Here the trail descends very steeply into the drainage and, just as quickly, climbs back out. At the top the trail forks.

Taking the trail to the right, following white marks and notchings on trees, you will come to an old, small cement tank where pipe is being connected for water. Continue past this and the trail will turn into a graded road. Follow this road for about 1/3 mile until you arrive at two 10-foot alligator juniper posts on the right, with wires hung between them. Turn left here, and again the trail starts down with a cairn on the right. The trail is very easy from here to Pine Trailhead, which is now very close.

*Dripping Springs on the Pine Canyon Trail—hiking anyone?*

# SEE CANYON TRAIL #184

**ATTRACTION:** Breathtaking scenery, lots of lush moss-covered flora, nice area for pictures.

**REQUIREMENTS:** Food, water, sturdy boots, proper maps; car okay to trailhead; 1.5 hours hiking time one way.

**LOCATION:** Payson Ranger District, west of Woods Canyon Lake.

**DIFFICULTY:** Moderate

**ELEVATIONS:** 7880' - 5894'

**LENGTH:** 4 miles one way.

**MAPS REQUIRED:** U.S.G.S. 7.5 min. topographic for Promontory Butte.

**PERMIT:** No    **BIKES:** Yes    **EQUESTRIAN:** Yes

**WATER:** Not dependable - bring your own.

**INFORMATION:** Trail rocky some areas; watch for cairns through vague areas.

**FIREARMS:** Yes    **PETS ON LEASH:** Yes

## TRAIL INFORMATION

Access to See Canyon trailhead is gained by taking State Route 260 east out of Payson for 50 miles where a left turn is made onto Forest Road #300. This is a gravel road but is fit for automobiles. After leaving Route 260, watch for trailhead sign in 12.3 miles on left side of road.

At the start of this breathtaking trail, a beauty develops around you that does not exist on any other trail in the system. You will be especially taken in by the many flowing tributaries the trail crosses. Also, there is the smell of clean, fresh air, not to mention the lush greenery, including the moss on the live and dead trees as well as on the rocks. It makes you feel as if you have visited an area that time has forgotten. About 1/2 mile from the intersection with Highline Trail #31 is a spur trail on the left leading to See Spring, approximately 1/2 mile in length. The water seeps from the ground under the very rocks on which you walk.

The real beauty is in the See Canyon Trail itself. It is a most inspiring trail!

# SEE CANYON TRAIL #184

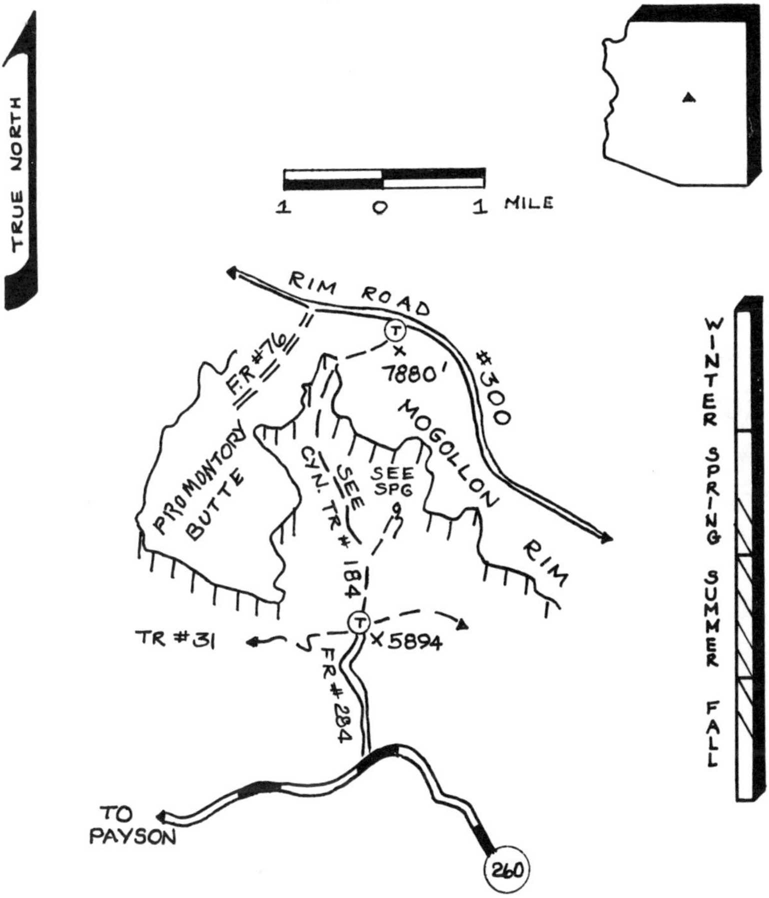

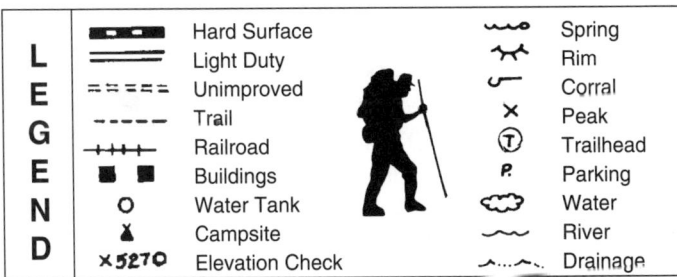

Hiking Central Arizona / 71

# ABBEY'S WAY TRAIL #151

**ATTRACTION:** Trail is surrounded by beautiful, mixed conifer forest; views from Aztec Peak lookout tower (when accessible).

**REQUIREMENTS:** Food, water, sturdy boots, proper maps; car okay to trailhead; 1.5 hours hiking time one way.

**LOCATION:** Pleasant Valley Ranger District - Aztec Peak.

**DIFFICULTY:** Difficult

**ELEVATIONS:** 6900' - 7720'

**LENGTH:** 2 miles one way

**MAPS REQUIRED:** U.S.G.S. 7.5 min. topographic for Aztec Peak.

**PERMIT:** No

**BIKES:** No

**EQUESTRIAN:** Yes

**WATER:** Not dependable - bring your own.

**INFORMATION:** The meadow which the trail borders is very susceptible to damage; please keep horses out. Trail is strenuous at high altitude.

**FIREARMS:** Yes

**PETS ON LEASH:** Yes

## TRAIL INFORMATION

Abbey's Way Trail leaves Forest Road 487 to the northeast and heads towards a mountain meadow which was part of an old homestead. The trail then climbs directly up the pine and Douglas fir-covered slopes of Aztec Peak towards the lookout tower. It includes some switchbacks near the top. The trail wraps around the peak and meets Forest Road 487 just east of the top of the peak.

# ABBEY'S WAY TRAIL #151

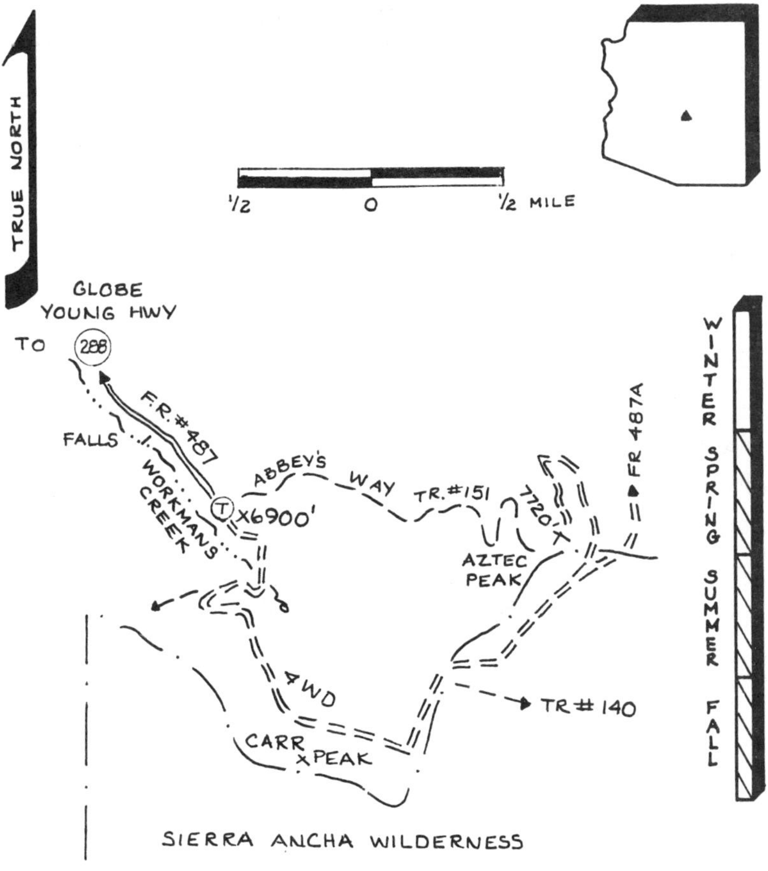

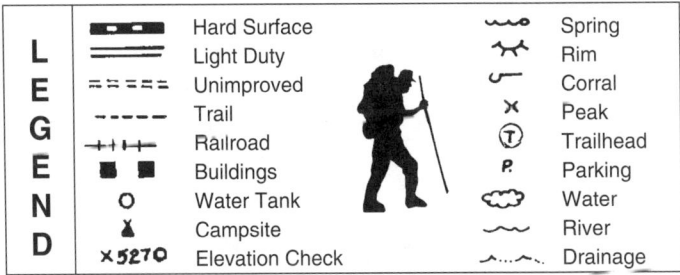

Hiking Central Arizona / 73

# DAN'S TRAIL #550

**ATTRACTION:** Trail is located near Valentine Ridge Campground and is excellent for all-terrain biking.

**REQUIREMENTS:** Food, water, sturdy boots, proper maps; car okay to trailhead; 2 hours hiking time one way.

**LOCATION:** Pleasant Valley Ranger District, southwest of Valentine Ridge Campground.

**DIFFICULTY:** Difficult

**ELEVATIONS:** 6720' - 7120'

**LENGTH:** 4.8 miles round trip

**MAPS REQUIRED:** U.S.G.S. 7.5 min. topographic for Parallel Canyon (Young NE).

**PERMIT:** No

**BIKES:** Yes - trail is adopted by the Mountain Bike Association of Arizona.

**EQUESTRIAN:** No

**WATER:** Not dependable - bring your own.

**INFORMATION:** Makes an excellent round trip loop with some road travel; be sure to pay attention and follow rock cairns.

**FIREARMS:** Yes

**PETS ON LEASH:** Yes

## TRAIL INFORMATION

**West End:** Take Forest Road #109, 2 1/4 miles southwest of Valentine Ridge Campground and 1/2 mile east of FR #512 (Young Highway).

**East End:** Take FR #109, 1 1/2 miles east of West terminus.

From Forest Road #109, Dan's Trail follows a ridge south for 2 miles with a 400-foot descent. It meets with Forest Road #512 at an arroyo bottom, then turns north to climb along another ridge. After 1 mile, it turns to the east and descends to another arroyo. It then turns north up a third ridge, to return to Forest Road #109 at a point 1 1/2 miles east of the trailhead.

A loop can be made by returning on Forest Road #109.

# DAN'S TRAIL #550

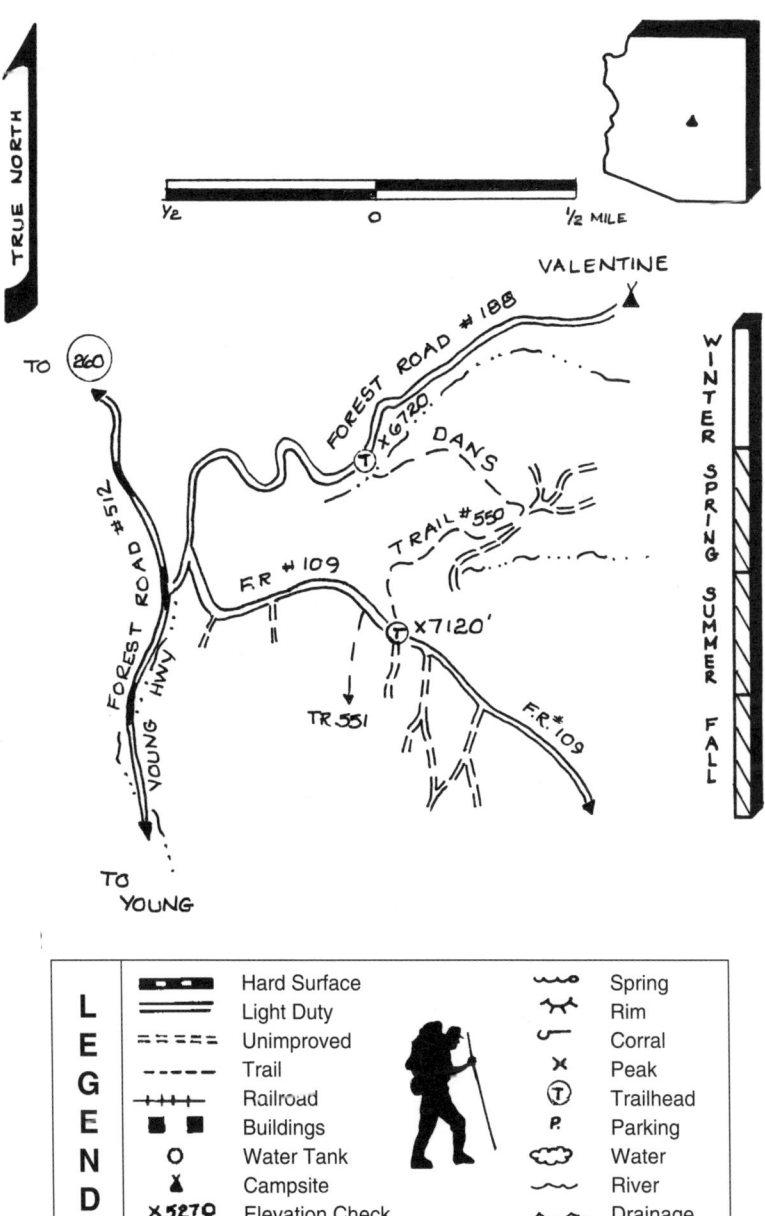

# MURPHY RANCH TRAIL #141

**ATTRACTION:** Access to Sierra Ancha Wilderness, lots of wildlife.

**REQUIREMENTS:** Food, water, sturdy boots, proper maps; car okay to trailhead; 1.5 hours hiking time round trip.

**LOCATION:** Pleasant Valley Ranger District - Aztec Peak area.

**DIFFICULTY:** Moderate

**ELEVATIONS:** 6740' - 7200'

**LENGTH:** 1.5 miles one way

**MAPS REQUIRED:** U.S.G.S. 7.5 min. topographic for Aztec Peak.

**PERMIT:** No

**BIKES:** No

**EQUESTRIAN:** Yes

**WATER:** Yes - Cold Springs Canyon.

**INFORMATION:** Murphy Ranch Trail dips down to Rim Trail; campsites at Murphy Ranch.

**FIREARMS:** Yes

**PETS ON LEASH:** Yes

## TRAIL INFORMATION

Take Route 88 north out of Claypool to Route 288 (Young Road) and continue to Forest Development Road (FDR) #487, then 6.5 miles to FDR #487A at Murphy Ranch. Murphy Ranch trailhead is about 100 feet from the ranch gate or from the Rim Trail #139 sign. This ranch is private property.

You will find easy hiking from the trailhead down to Rim Trail. If you study your maps, you can build on your hike from Rim Trail.

Part of this trail, located outside the Sierra Ancha Wilderness, was an old logging road.

# MURPHY RANCH TRAIL #141

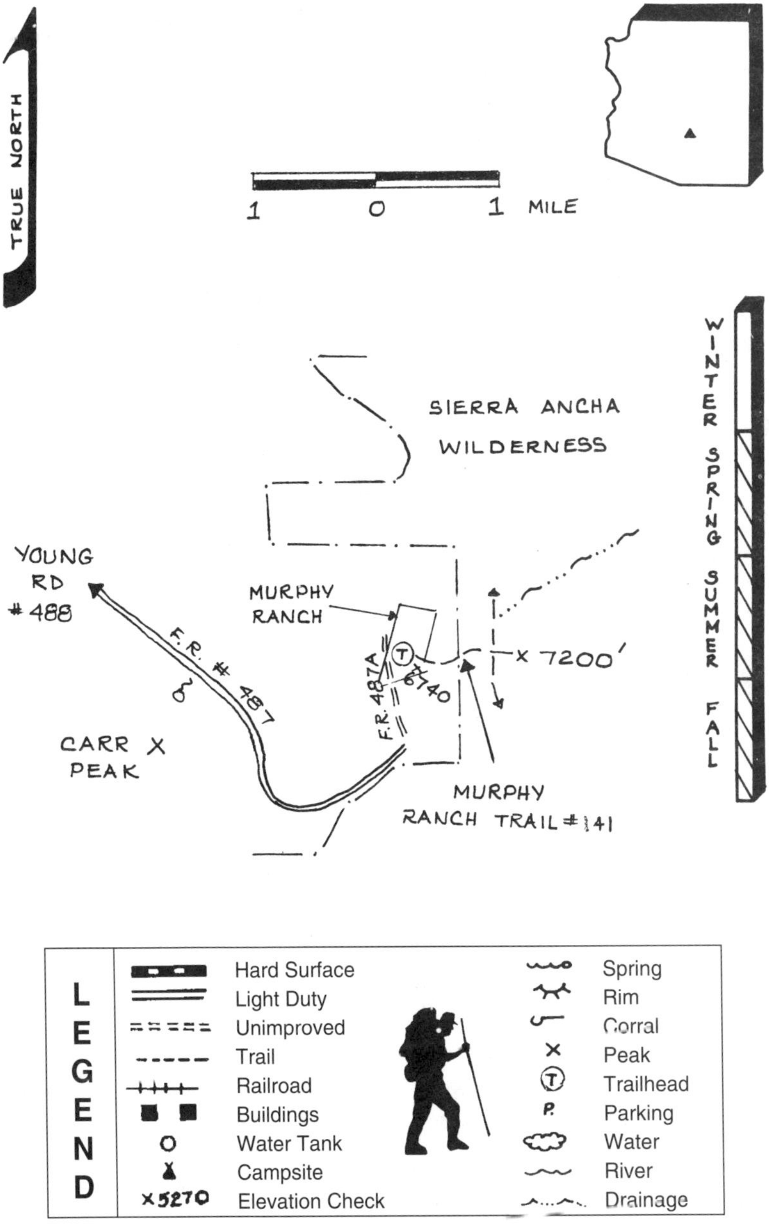

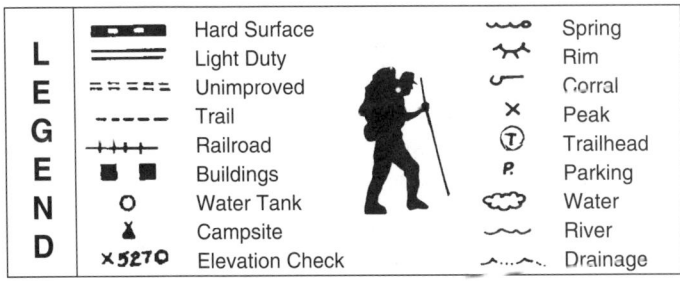

Hiking Central Arizona / 77

# PARKER CREEK TRAIL #160

**ATTRACTION:** Four vegetation types to hike through, unusual geological features, views across to Armer Mountain.

**REQUIREMENTS:** Food, water, sturdy boots, proper maps; car okay to trailhead; 3.5 hours hiking time one way.

**LOCATION:** Pleasant Valley Ranger District - Parker Creek Experimental Station.

**DIFFICULTY:** Moderate

**ELEVATIONS:** 5080' - 7080'   **LENGTH:** 4 miles one way.

**MAPS REQUIRED:** U.S.G.S. 7.5 min. topographic for Aztec Peak.

**PERMIT:** No   **BIKES:** No

**EQUESTRIAN:** Yes   **WATER:** Yes - Parker Creek.

**INFORMATION:** Be sure to pace yourself; look for insulators from old telegraph lines; remember, this is bear country!

**FIREARMS:** Yes   **PETS ON LEASH:** Yes

## TRAIL INFORMATION

Take Route 60 east to Route 88 just outside Claypool and turn left. Take Route 88 to Route 288 (Young Road), turn right and continue for 29 miles (10 are unpaved but in good condition.)

When you arrive at the sign indicating Sierra Ancha Experimental Forest, continue on about 300 feet where a small road goes to the right leading to the station. A short distance up the road, it will be blocked to vehicles, but there is ample room to park.

Continue walking up the road, past the gate, and turn right at the first "T" in the road. Then 150 feet further, you will be at the trailhead. The trail is in excellent condition and ample in width, with many switchbacks to help you on your way. *But one must take care on this trail—it is a long roll to the bottom in many places.*

Although this trail does not go to Aztec Peak, your stopping point on a high, flat plateau leaves you only 614 feet short of its summit in altitude; however, you're still a good quarter-mile away.

Along the way, you will encounter four types of vegetation, three rocky slopes, numerous pinnacle and geological formations, including spectacular views of Roosevelt Lake and the Four Peaks Wilderness area. Trail ends at the junction with Rim Trail #139.

# PARKER CREEK TRAIL #160

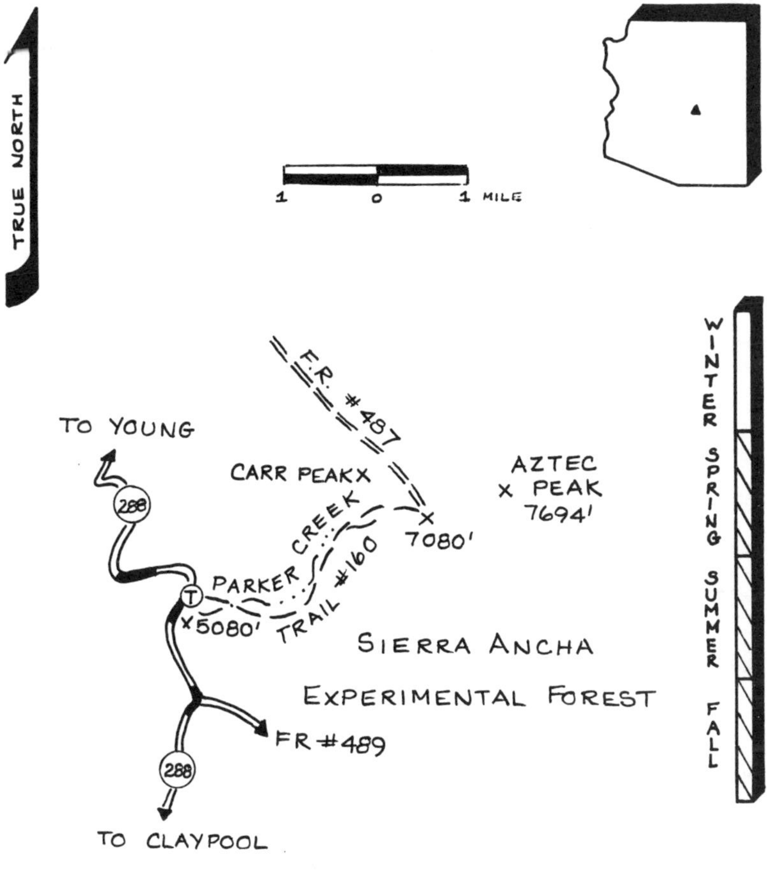

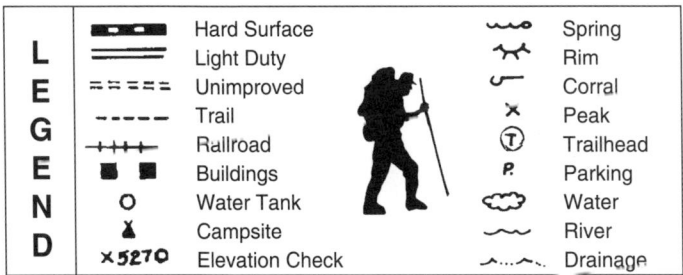

Hiking Central Arizona / 79

# RIM TRAIL #139

**ATTRACTION:** Very scenic views looking over Rim to the south; this trail connects many other trails.

**REQUIREMENTS:** Food, water, sturdy boots, proper maps; car okay to trailhead; 3.5 hours hiking time one way.

**LOCATION:** Pleasant Valley Ranger District - Aztec Peak.

**DIFFICULTY:** Moderate

**ELEVATIONS:** 6400' - 6800'

**LENGTH:** 7.6 miles one way.

**MAPS REQUIRED:** U.S.G.S. 7.5 min. topographic for Aztec Peak.

**PERMIT:** No

**BIKES:** No

**EQUESTRIAN:** Yes

**WATER:** Not dependable - bring your own.

**INFORMATION:** Campsites and water at Hunt Spring and Edwards Spring. More water possible at Cold Springs Canyon.

**FIREARMS:** Yes

**PETS ON LEASH:** Yes

## TRAIL INFORMATION

Take Route 88 north out of Miami for approximately 15 miles to the junction with Route 288. Travel north on 288 at Forest Road 487, past Workman Falls to Murphy Ranch Road (Forest Road 246) following FR 246 just under a mile to the Murphy Ranch gate. Park and proceed on Murphy Ranch Trail #141. Proceed to Rim Trail intersection, turn south here and, in about 1/3 mile, you will join Moody Point Trail. Shortly, Rim Trail will again take off by itself to its terminus at Forest Road 487.

Know your map as this trail can be hard to follow at times.

It works well to car shuttle from the terminus (FR 487) to the beginning trailhead at Murphy Ranch.

# RIM TRAIL #139

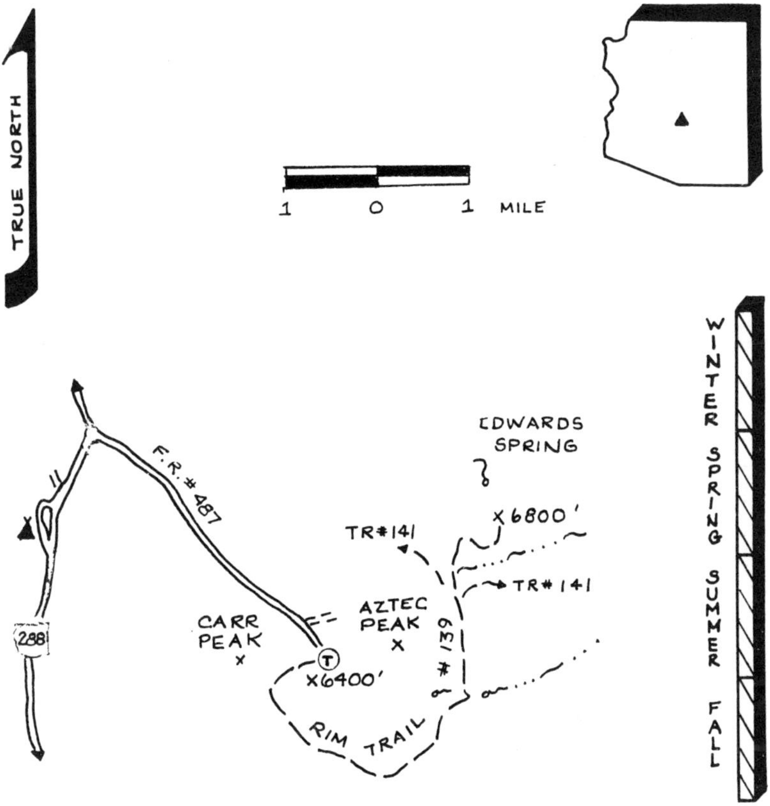

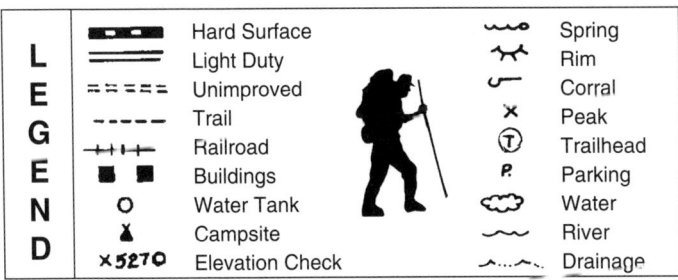

Hiking Central Arizona / 81

# BEAR CANYON TRAIL #299

**ATTRACTION:** Nice views, cool hiking.

**REQUIREMENTS:** Food, water, sturdy boots, proper maps; car okay to trailhead; 3 hours hiking time one way.

**LOCATION:** Safford Ranger District - Piñaleno Mountains.

**DIFFICULTY:** Difficult

**ELEVATIONS:** 8780' - 4920'

**LENGTH:** 6 miles one way

**MAPS REQUIRED:** U.S.G.S. 7.5 min. topographic for Stockton Pass.

**PERMIT:** No

**BIKES:** No

**EQUESTRIAN:** Yes

**WATER:** No - bring your own.

**INFORMATION:** You might consider a car shuttle to avoid hike back. Be alert, this is bear country.

**FIREARMS:** Yes

**PETS ON LEASH:** Yes

## TRAIL INFORMATION

Take Highway 366 south of Safford 17 miles to Ladybug Saddle, adjacent to Highway 366, Swift Trail.

Park at saddle and start hike. Trail heads due east but, in just a short distance, will head south for remainder of the hike.

At .5 mile is a junction where a left turn would take you to Ladybug Peak. In only .1 mile more is another junction; the trail to your left is Ladybug Trail #329. At the 1-mile mark is yet another junction where a left turn becomes Dutch Henry Trail #297; a right turn here keeps you on Bear Canyon Trail.

In just over 1 mile more is the last junction where a trail to the left leads to a helispot. The Bear Canyon Trail now descends the next 3.5 miles to its end at Highway 266.

# BEAR CANYON TRAIL #299

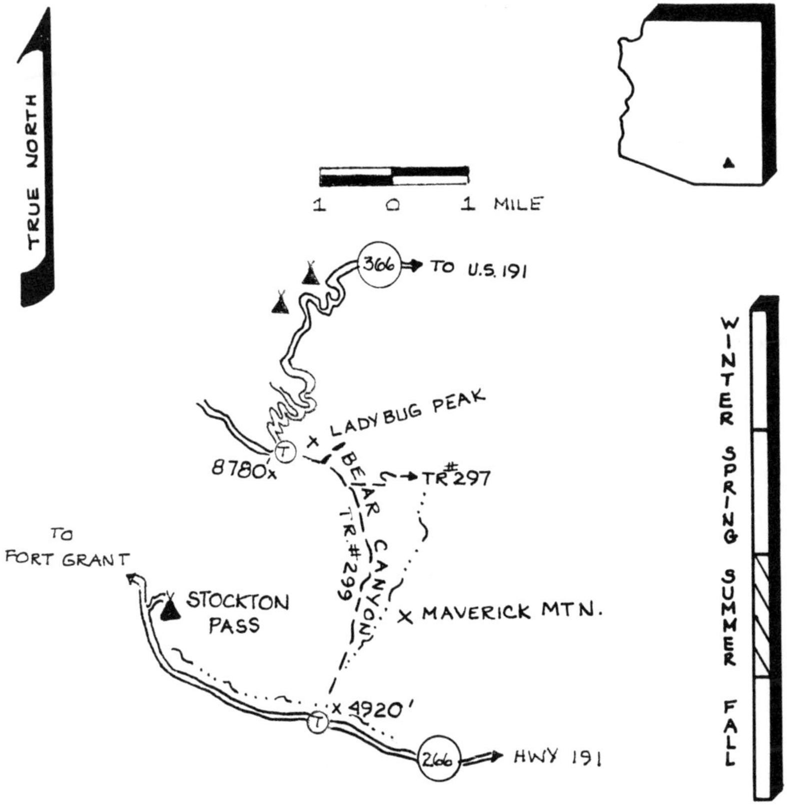

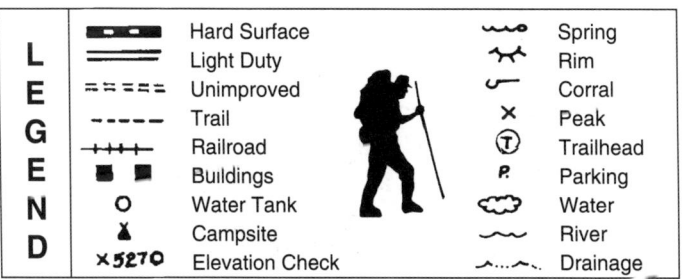

# FRYE CANYON TRAIL #36

**ATTRACTION:** Nice views.

**REQUIREMENTS:** Food, water, sturdy boots, proper maps; pickup to trailhead; 3 hours hiking time one way.

**LOCATION:** Safford Ranger District, southwest of Thatcher.

**DIFFICULTY:** Difficult

**ELEVATIONS:** 5350' - 7120'

**LENGTH:** 2.8 miles one way.

**MAPS REQUIRED:** U.S.G.S. 7.5 min. topographic for Mt. Graham.

**PERMIT:** No

**BIKES:** No

**EQUESTRIAN:** Yes

**WATER:** Yes, at Frye Creek, but best to bring your own.

**INFORMATION:** Bring lots of water and pace yourself.

**FIREARMS:** Yes

**PETS ON LEASH:** Yes

## TRAIL INFORMATION

From Stadium Road out of Thatcher, take Forest Road #103 to Frye Mesa. Forest Road #103 from the bottom of the mesa to the top is not recommended for passenger cars.

The Frye Canyon Trail starts at Frye Mesa beyond the reservoir turnoff and terminates at its junction with the Round-The-Mountain Trail #302 in just under 3 miles. The junction is called Inception and is the site of an old ranger station. For the most part the trail follows Frye Creek. Return the way you came.

# FRYE CANYON TRAIL #36

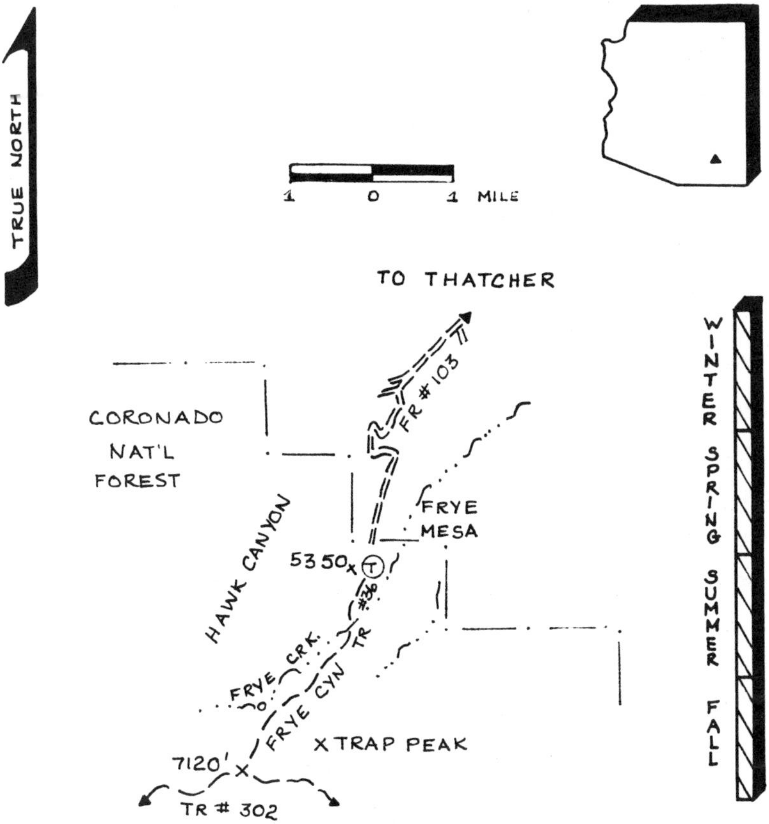

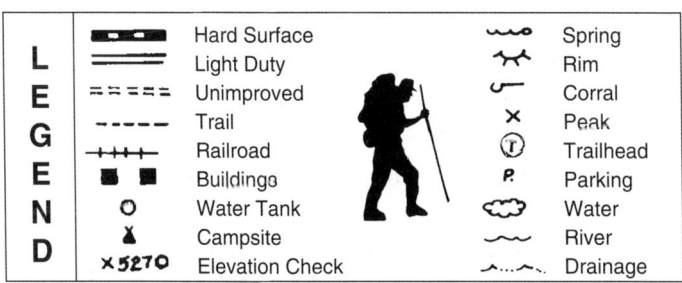

| LEGEND | | | | |
|---|---|---|---|---|
| ▬▬▬ | Hard Surface | | ∽∽∽o | Spring |
| ═══ | Light Duty | | ⌖ | Rim |
| ═ ═ ═ | Unimproved | | ⌒ | Corral |
| ----- | Trail | | × | Peak |
| ┼┼┼┼ | Railroad | | Ⓣ | Trailhead |
| ■ ■ | Buildings | | P. | Parking |
| O | Water Tank | | ⌒⌒ | Water |
| ⛺ | Campsite | | ∽∽ | River |
| ×5270 | Elevation Check | | ∽...∽. | Drainage |

*Hiking Central Arizona* / 85

# GRANT GOUDY RIDGE TRAIL #310

**ATTRACTION:** Wonderful views of Greasewood Mountains and Sulpher Springs Valley.

**REQUIREMENTS:** Food, water, sturdy boots, proper maps; car okay to trailhead; 4.5 hours hiking time one way.

**LOCATION:** Safford Ranger District - Soldier Creek Campground.

**DIFFICULTY:** Difficult - long way down.

**ELEVATIONS:** 9500' - 5000'

**LENGTH:** 8 miles one way

**MAPS REQUIRED:** U.S.G.S. 7.5 min. topographic for Webb Peak.

**PERMIT:** No

**BIKES:** No

**EQUESTRIAN:** Yes

**WATER:** Only at campground.

**INFORMATION:** Consider a car shuttle to avoid long hike back up. Be alert; this is bear country.

**FIREARMS:** Yes

**PETS ON LEASH:** Yes

## TRAIL INFORMATION

Trailhead is located at Soldier Creek Campground off Swift Trail (Highway 366). Forest Road #656 turns south off Swift Trail to Soldier Creek Campground.

Heading south out of the campground, and always descending for the next 8 miles, you will go through vegetation changes from mixed conifer to oak woodland, and then into the desert and the valley floor. This hike affords wonderful chances to see a wide variety of Arizona critters.

The trail terminates at the end of Forest Road #157, just over 2 miles north of Fort Grant Industrial School.

# GRANT GOUDY RIDGE
# TRAIL #310

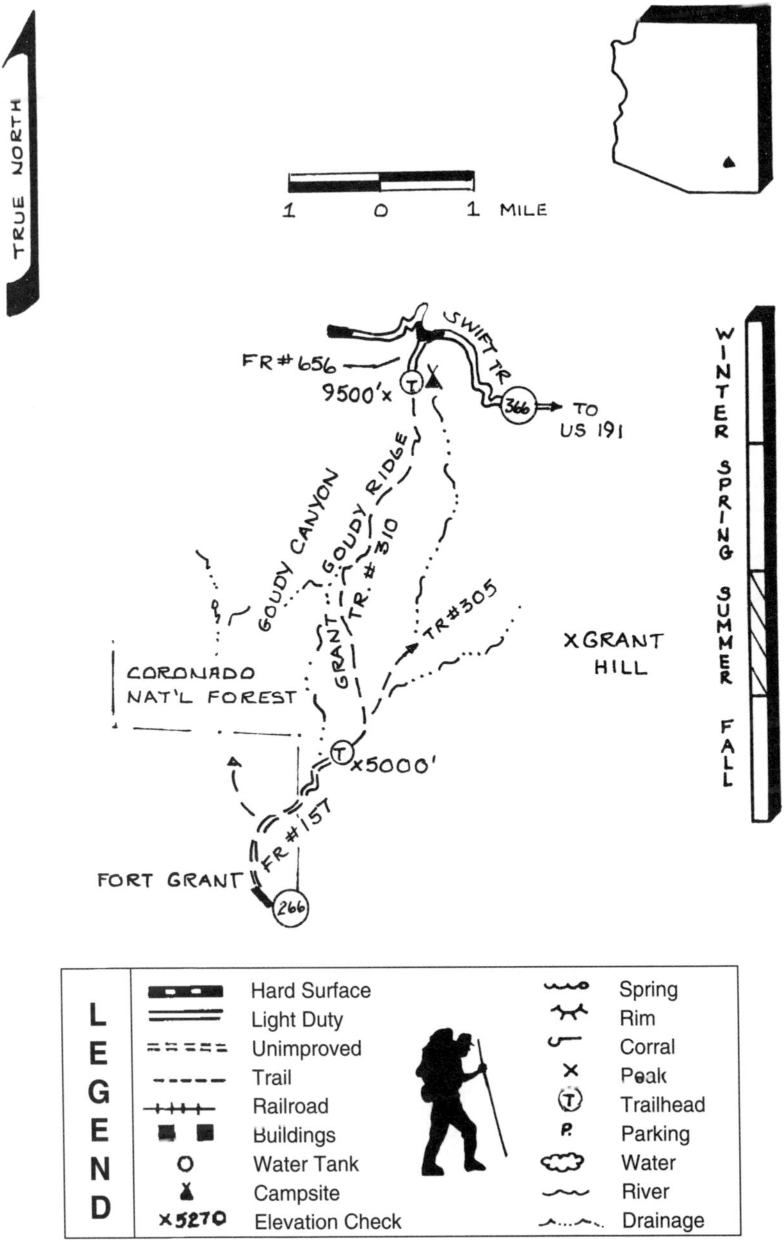

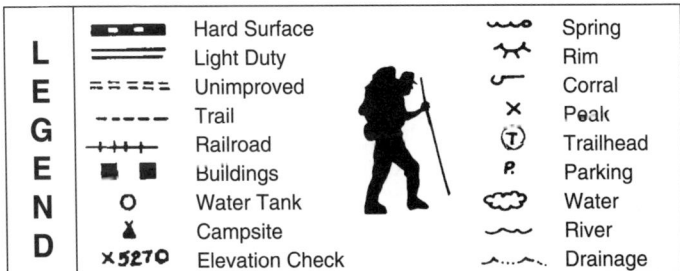

# LADYBUG TRAIL #329

**ATTRACTION:** Great views, a nice variety of scenery.

**REQUIREMENTS:** Food, water, sturdy boots, proper maps; car okay to trailhead; 3 hours hiking time one way.

**LOCATION:** Safford Ranger District - Piñaleno Mountains.

**DIFFICULTY:** Moderate

**ELEVATIONS:** 8780' - 5200'

**LENGTH:** 5.9 miles one way

**MAPS REQUIRED:** U.S.G.S. 7.5 min. topographic for Stockton Pass.

**PERMIT:** No

**BIKES:** No

**EQUESTRIAN:** Yes

**WATER:** No - bring your own.

**INFORMATION:** Consider a car shuttle to avoid the long hike back. Be alert, this is bear country.

**FIREARMS:** Yes

**PETS ON LEASH:** Yes

## TRAIL INFORMATION

Follow all directions to the trailhead of Bear Canyon Trail #229. Then follow Bear Canyon Trail itself 1/2 mile to its junction with Ladybug Trail.

From this junction, the trail is 5.9 miles long, crossing Jacobson Ridge and ending at Angle Orchard. You are likely to see signs of bear and deer on the trail. The lower vegetation will change to oak woodland and then to scrub and manzanita near the orchard.

# LADYBUG TRAIL #329

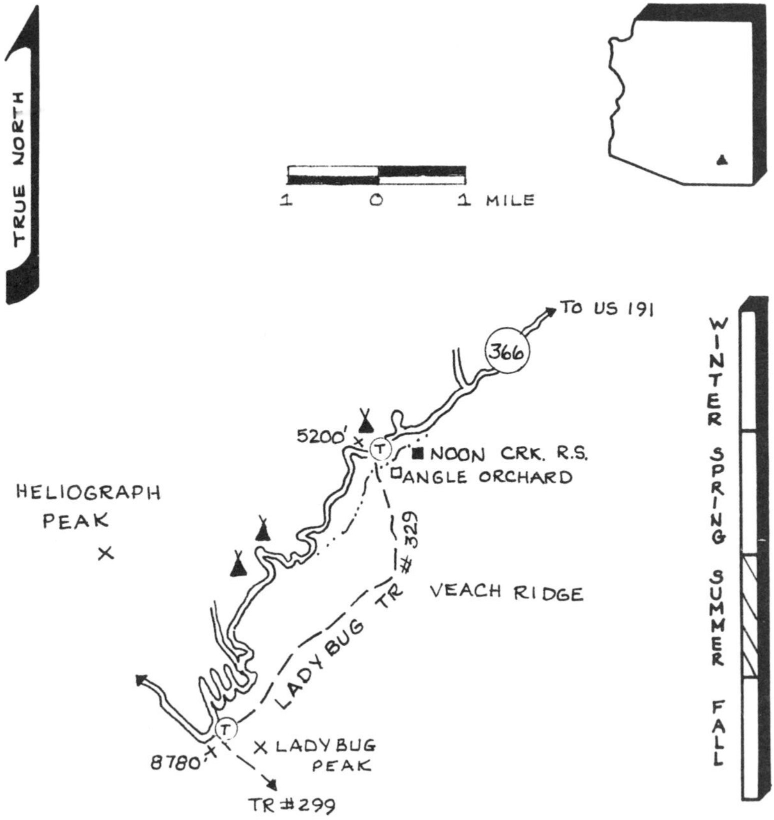

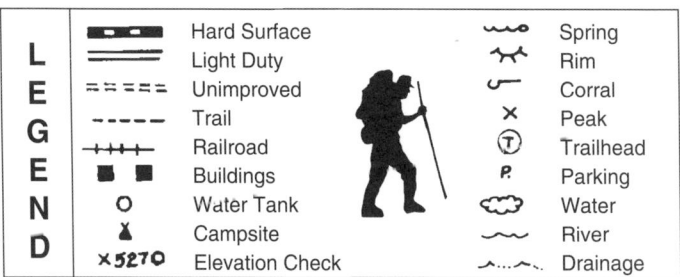

*Hiking Central Arizona* / 89

# SHAKE TRAIL #309

**ATTRACTION:** Wonderful views of Greasewood Mountains and Sulpher Springs Valley.

**REQUIREMENTS:** Food, water, sturdy boots, proper maps; car okay to trailhead; 2 hours hiking time one way.

**LOCATION:** Safford Ranger District - Piñaleno Mountains.

**DIFFICULTY:** Moderate

**ELEVATIONS:** 8500' - 5500'

**LENGTH:** 4.8 miles one way.

**MAPS REQUIRED:** U.S.G.S. 7.5 min. topographic for Stockton Pass.

**PERMIT:** No

**BIKES:** No

**EQUESTRIAN:** Yes

**WATER:** Yes, but best to bring your own.

**INFORMATION:** Consider a car shuttle to avoid the long hike back up. Remember, this is bear country.

**FIREARMS:** Yes

**PETS ON LEASH:** Yes

## TRAIL INFORMATION

Follow directions to Ladybug Saddle in the Trail Information for Bear Canyon Trail #299.

This trail starts 1/2 mile west of Ladybug Saddle at 8500 feet, and descends through oak woodland to 5500 feet at Stockton Pass near Stockton Pass Campground. There is potable water here.

The upper trailhead is accessible from the middle of May through November. During winter months one could hike from Stockton Pass up to the snow and return.

# SHAKE TRAIL #309

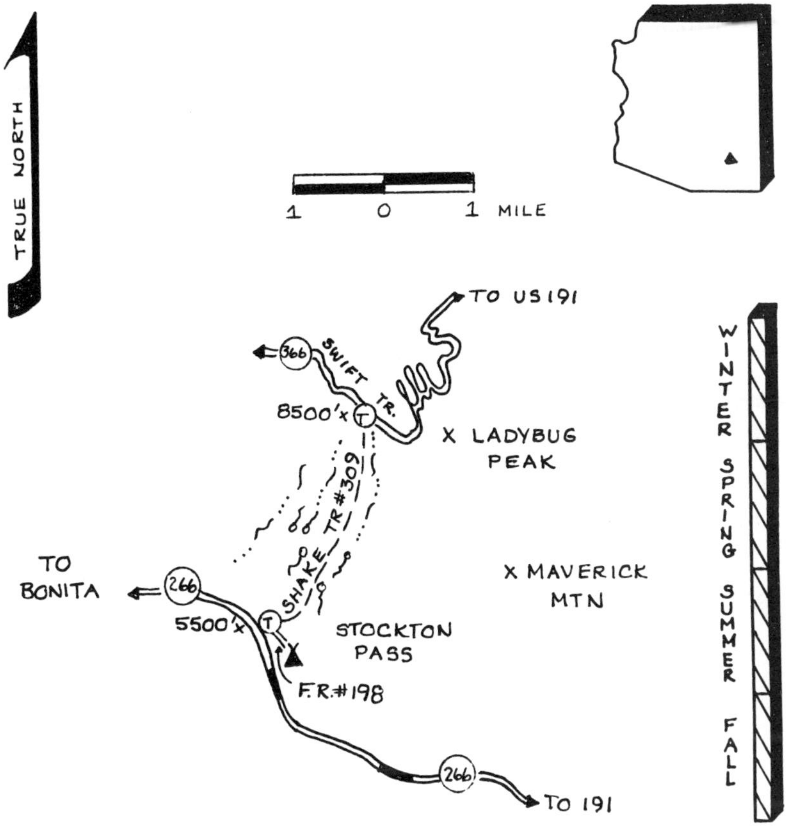

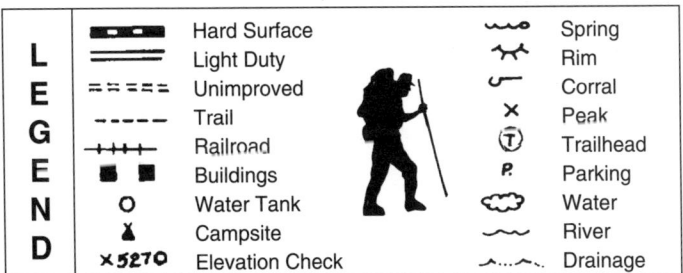

Hiking Central Arizona / 91

# BLACK MESA TRAIL #241

**ATTRACTION:** Nice views of Weaver's Needle.

**REQUIREMENTS:** Food, water, sturdy boots, proper maps; car okay to trailhead with care; 6 hours hiking time round trip.

**LOCATION:** Tonto Basin Ranger District - Superstition Mountains.

**DIFFICULTY:** Moderate

**ELEVATIONS:** 2270' - 2750'

**LENGTH:** 5.5 miles one way

**MAPS REQUIRED:** U.S.G.S. 7.5 min. topographic for Goldfield.

**PERMIT:** No    **BIKES:** No

**EQUESTRIAN:** Yes    **WATER:** No - bring your own.

**INFORMATION:** Trail can be hard to follow in some areas. Nice loop trail via Dutchmans Trail #104.

**FIREARMS:** Yes    **PETS ON LEASH:** Yes

## TRAIL INFORMATION

Drive north from Apache Junction on Highway 88 approximately 5.3 miles to Forest Road #78 (First Water Rd.). Turn right and follow this road for 2.6 miles to trailhead. If you have a trailer, park 1/2 mile before the trailhead. Start on foot from gate.

Approximately 1/4 mile from the gate at a fork, Dutchman's Trail #104 will take off to the right. In only a stone's throw more, Second Water Trail #236 takes off to the left. Turn left here and follow the main trail closely. After climbing, you will again lose altitude towards a wash, climb again and, at about the 1 1/2-mile mark, end up at Garden Valley. Hiking across the valley for about 1/4 mile, keep a close eye out for Black Mesa Trailhead on the right and turn here. Do not travel straight on Second Water Trail.

Gradually climbing now, you will be above Garden Valley with Weaver's Needle in the distance. Trail will level out and, for the next 2 miles, you must take your time to be sure you stay on the trail. In about 2 miles you will be at the junction of Dutchman's Trail #104 and end of Black Mesa Trail. A right turn here on Dutchman's Trail will take you back to where you started. (See Dutchman's Trail #104.)

# BLACK MESA TRAIL #241

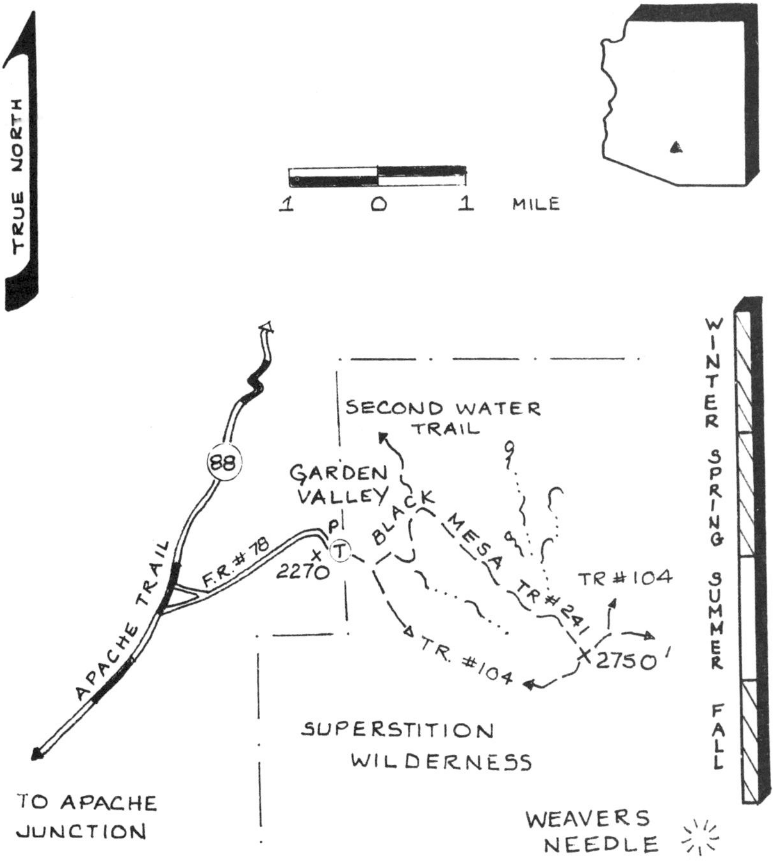

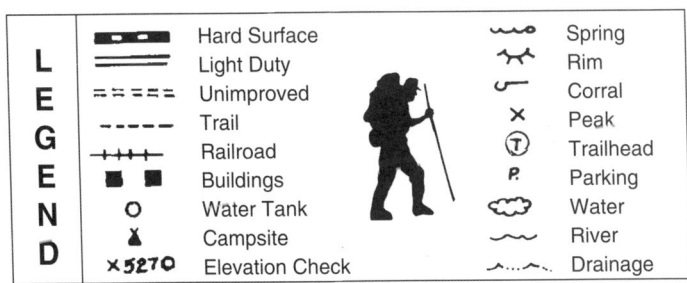

# DUTCHMAN'S TRAIL #104

**ATTRACTION:** Good condition, nice scenery.

**REQUIREMENTS:** Food, water, sturdy boots, proper maps; car okay to trailhead with care; 5 hours hiking time round trip.

**LOCATION:** Tonto Basin Ranger District - Superstition Mountains.

**DIFFICULTY:** Moderate

**ELEVATIONS:** 2270' - 2750'

**LENGTH:** 4.5 miles one way to junction with trail #241 for loop hike on Black Mesa Trail.

**MAPS REQUIRED:** U.S.G.S. 7.5 min. topographic for Goldfield.

**PERMIT:** No

**BIKES:** No

**EQUESTRIAN:** Yes

**WATER:** Yes, but purify.

**INFORMATION:** Trail #104 is 18.2 miles long and terminates at Peralta trailhead. I have used only 4.5 miles for loop hike.

**FIREARMS:** Yes

**PETS ON LEASH:** Yes

## TRAIL INFORMATION

Follow directions to trailhead for Black Mesa Trail #241. Approximately 1/4 mile from the gate, Dutchman's Trail #104 will take off to the right.

As you meander along First Water Creek in the early part of the hike, it will be no mystery that this was mining country in the past. Soon you will leave the creek and climb a bit as you travel through Parker Pass and Boulder Canyon to the junction of Black Mesa Trail #241. A left turn here on trail #241 will take you back to where you started. (See Black Mesa Trail #241.)

# DUTCHMAN'S TRAIL #104

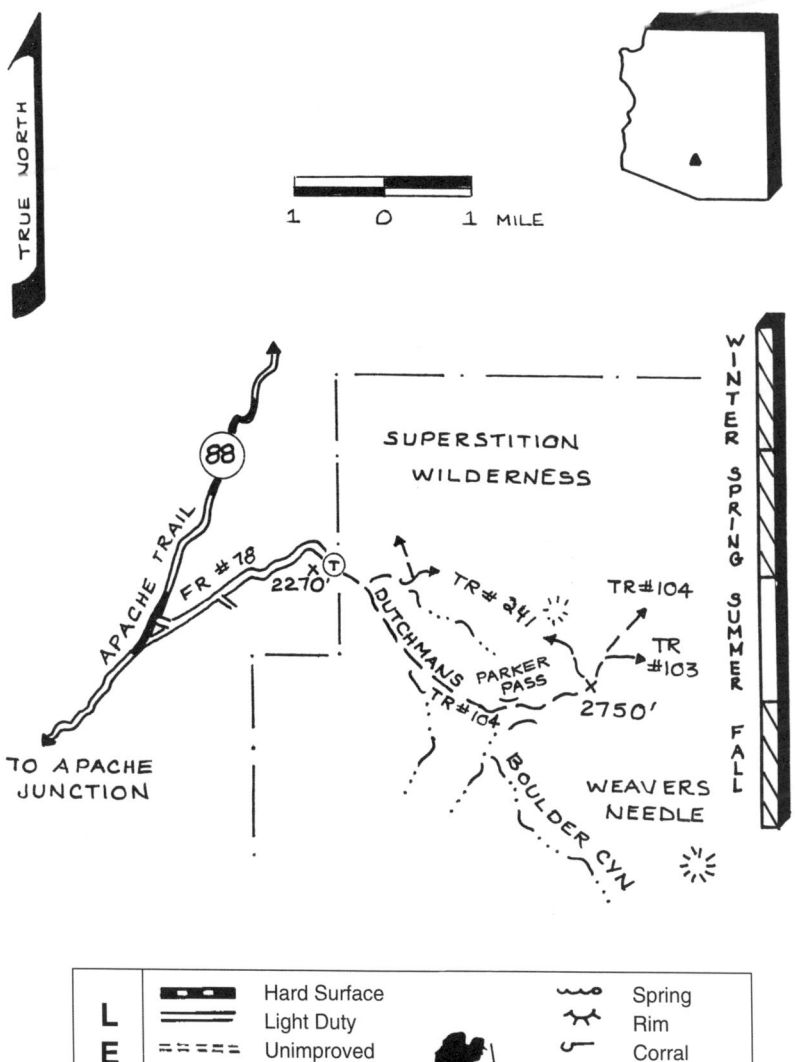

*Hiking Central Arizona* / 95

# JUG TRAIL #61

**ATTRACTION:** Wildlife sightings very possible due to water access.

**REQUIREMENTS:** Water, food, sturdy boots, proper maps; car okay to trailhead; 1 hour hiking time one way.

**LOCATION:** Tonto Basin Ranger District, north end of Roosevelt Lake.

**DIFFICULTY:** Moderate

**ELEVATIONS:** 2800' - 3300'

**LENGTH:** 2 miles one way

**MAPS REQUIRED:** U.S.G.S. 7.5 min. topographic for Green Back Creek and Armer Mountain.

**PERMIT:** No

**BIKES:** No

**EQUESTRIAN:** Yes

**WATER:** Yes - but best to bring your own.

**INFORMATION:** Use caution along the creek.

**FIREARMS:** Yes

**PETS ON LEASH:** Yes - leash preferred.

## TRAIL INFORMATION

Trail begins on Forest Road 60, the "A-Cross Road" which begins near the north end of Roosevelt Lake on State Route 188. There is a semi-primitive trailhead and parking for only a few cars.

Trail provides access to Salome Wilderness. The trail was converted from an old road so it is fairly wide and follows an easy grade. The trail ends before it reaches Salome Creek. From the terminus, hikers may select their own route to the creek, but caution is urged due to many natural hazards which may be encountered along the creek, such as swift currents, cliffs, and uneven terrain.

# JUG TRAIL #61

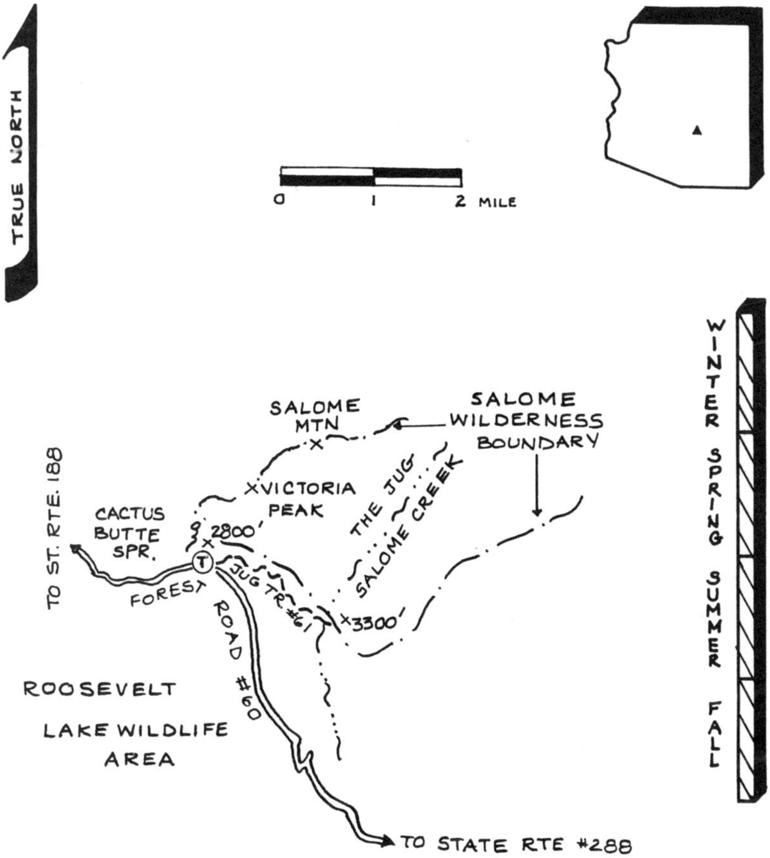

Hiking Central Arizona / 97

# REAVIS GAP TRAIL #117

**ATTRACTION:** A true wilderness experience as well as, at times, a real challenge.

**REQUIREMENTS:** Water, snack, sturdy boots, proper maps; car okay to trailhead; 1 hour hiking time one way.

**LOCATION:** Tonto Basin Ranger District, near Roosevelt Estates and entirely within the Superstition Wilderness area.

**DIFFICULTY:** Difficult

**ELEVATIONS:** 3400' - 4800'

**LENGTH:** 1.7 miles one way

**MAPS REQUIRED:** U.S.G.S. 7.5 min. topographic for Two Bar Mountain.

**PERMIT:** No

**BIKES:** No

**EQUESTRIAN:** Yes

**WATER:** Yes - best to bring your own.

**INFORMATION:** From Campaign Creek to Reavis Gap the trail is very steep due to the fact that it has no switchbacks.

**FIREARMS:** Yes

**PETS ON LEASH:** Yes

## TRAIL INFORMATION

Trailhead is located adjacent to the Reavis Mountain School at the end of Forest Road 449A. 449A branches off of Forest Road 449 which junctions with State Route 88 near Roosevelt Estates. Users access the trail via the Campaign Trail #256 which goes around the Reavis Mountain School. The Reavis Trail begins about 1/4 mile beyond the school.

The trail is entirely within the Superstition Wilderness. It begins by following a tributary of Campaign Creek. There is a fairly steep climb to Reavis Gap, at which point the trail passes out of the Tonto Basin District and into the Mesa District. The junction of Two Bar Ridge Trail #119 is located just west of Reavis Gap. The distance from the district boundary to the terminus at Reavis Ranch is approximately 3 miles.

# REAVIS GAP TRAIL #117

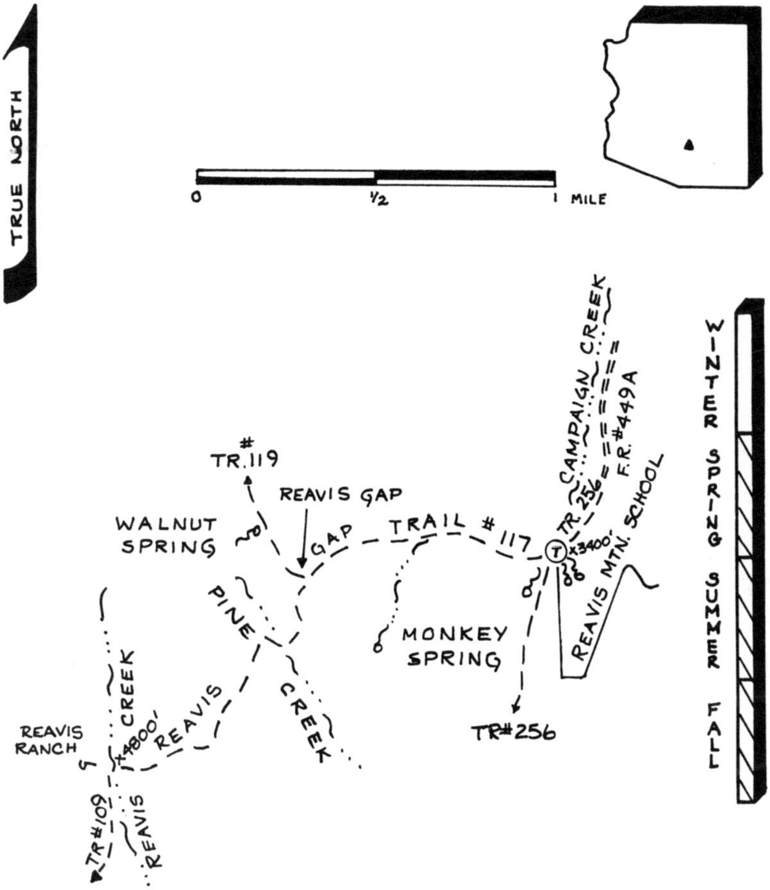

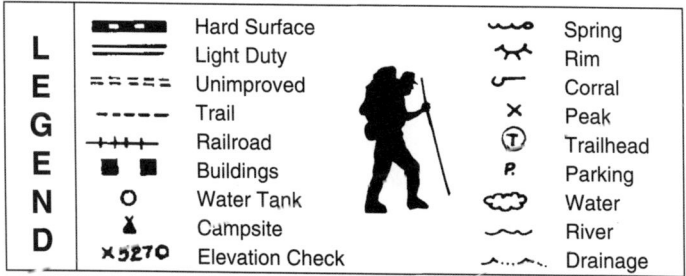

| L | ▬▬▬ | Hard Surface | ⌇⌇o | Spring |
| E | ▬▬▬ | Light Duty | ⌇⌇⌇ | Rim |
| G | ═ ═ ═ | Unimproved | ⌒ | Corral |
| E | - - - - | Trail | × | Peak |
| N | ┼┼┼┼ | Railroad | Ⓣ | Trailhead |
| D | ■ ■ | Buildings | P. | Parking |
|   | O | Water Tank | ⌬ | Water |
|   | ▲ | Campsite | ～ | River |
|   | ×5270 | Elevation Check | ⋯⋯ | Drainage |

*Hiking Central Arizona* / 99

# TULE CANYON TRAIL #122

**ATTRACTION:** Provides good access to the Eastern Superstition Wilderness.

**REQUIREMENTS:** Food, water, sturdy boots, proper maps; car okay to trailhead; 3 hours hiking time round trip.

**LOCATION:** Tonto Basin Ranger District - Superstition Mountains.

**DIFFICULTY:** Moderate

**ELEVATIONS:** 2800' - 4800'

**LENGTH:** 4.5 miles one way.

**MAPS REQUIRED:** U.S.G.S. 7.5 min. topographic for Two Bar Mountain.

**PERMIT:** No

**BIKES:** No

**EQUESTRIAN:** Yes

**WATER:** No - bring your own.

**INFORMATION:** Nice relocated trail.

**FIREARMS:** Yes

**PETS ON LEASH:** Yes

## TRAIL INFORMATION

Drive west from Globe on Highway 88 approximately 21.2 miles (from Highway 60 junction) to the Cross P Ranch Road #449 turnoff. Turn left and follow this road for approximately 2 miles to another road and turn right here. The trailhead will be in 3 miles; you will see a parking area on your right.

The trail heads southwest into Tule Canyon. About 1/3 of the way into the trail, after completing a half loop and now heading due west, you will enter the Superstition Wilderness. The trail will head northwest for a short time, which may seem wrong, but shortly you will head due south before again traveling due west to complete the trail.

This trail terminates at the junction of Two Bar Ridge Trail #119. Return the same way.

# TULE CANYON TRAIL #122

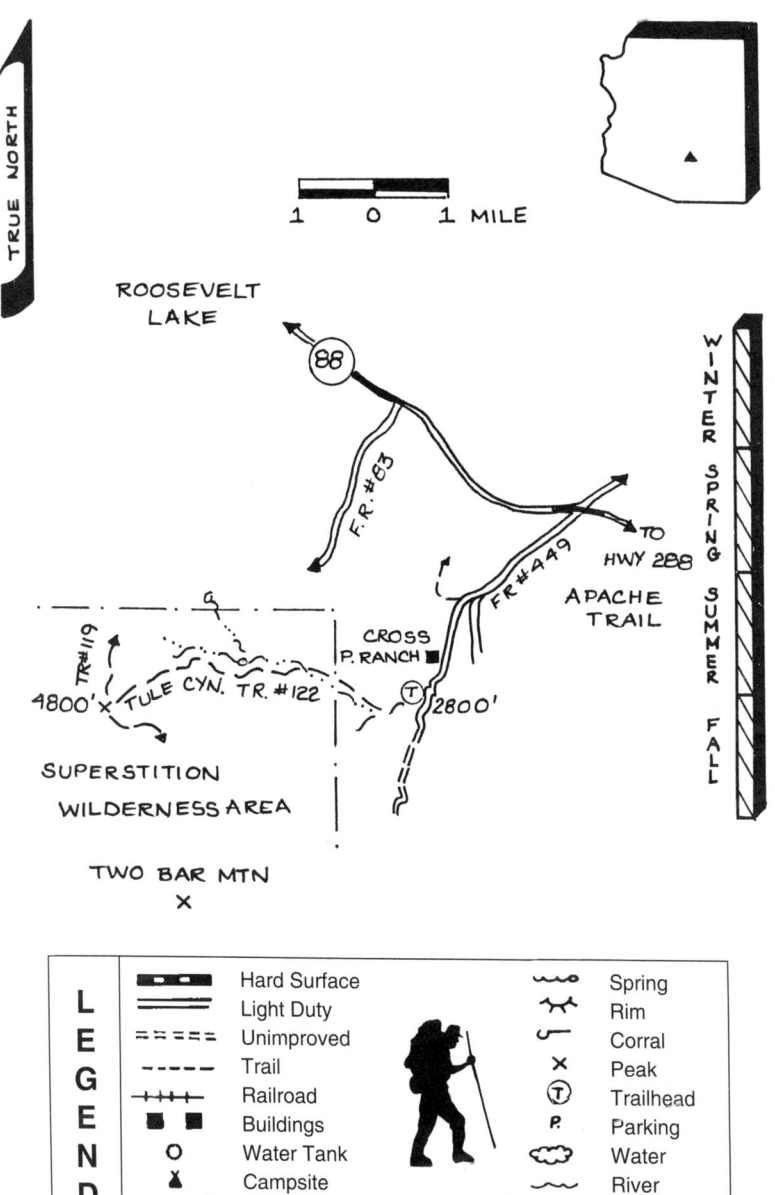

# HIKING CENTRAL ARIZONA RANGER DISTRICTS

Contact the following for more information:

**Cave Creek Ranger District**
Box 5068
Carefree, AZ 85377
602-488-3441
- Cave Creek Trail #4
- Palo Verde Trail #512
- Quien Sabe Trail #250
- Skull Mesa Trail #248
- Skunk Tank Trail #246

**Clifton Ranger District**
Box 698
Clifton, AZ 85533
520-687-1301
- East Eagle Trail #33
- Highline Trail #47
- Little Blue Creek Trail #41
- Raspberry Trail #35
- Strayhorse Canyon Trail #20

**Globe Ranger District**
R.R. 1, Box 31
Globe, AZ 88501
520-425-7189
- Icehouse Canyon Trail #198
- Kellner Canyon Trail #242
- Sixshooter Canyon Trail #197
- Squaw Spring Trail #196
- Telephone Trail #192

**Mesa Ranger District**
Box 5800
26 N. McDonald
Mesa, AZ 85211-5800
602-379-6446
- Amethyst Trail #253
- Browns Trail #133
- Four Peaks Trail #130
- Peralta Trail #102
- Pigeon Trail #134

**Payson Ranger District**
1009 E. Highway 260
Payson, AZ 85541
520-474-7900
- Babe Haught Trail #143
- Highline Trail #31
- Horton Creek Trail #285
- Pine Canyon Trail #26
- See Canyon Trail #184

**Pleasant Valley Ranger District**
Box 450
Young, AZ 85554
520-462-3311
- Abbey's Way Trail #151
- Dan's Trail #550
- Murphy Ranch Trail #141
- Parker Creek Trail #160
- Rim Trail #139

(Continued next page)

(Central Arizona Ranger Districts Continued)

**Safford Ranger District**
Box 709
Safford, AZ 85548-0709
520-428-4150
- Bear Canyon Trail #299
- Frye Canyon Trail #36
- Grant Goudy Ridge Trail #310
- Ladybug Trail #329
- Shake Trail #309

**Tonto Basin Ranger District**
Highway 88, Box 649
Roosevelt, AZ 85545
520-467-2236
- Black Mesa Trail #241
- Dutchman's Trail #104
- Jug Trail #61
- Reavis Gap Trail #117
- Tule Canyon Trail #122

# Weather—Great, but Changeable

The saying goes, if you don't like the weather in Arizona, then just wait a few minutes.

This is a fine example of how fast a change can occur and, depending on how far you are out on the trail, and if unprepared, can be the start of your demise.

Arizona's wide array of extremes from the hot arid desert to the cool (if not freezing) lofty peaks carries with it the perfect ingredients for you to be concerned—concerned enough to never travel unprepared!

July and August are the most unpredictable months. Fast growing storms in the mountains and on the desert can cause flash floods and severe drops in temperature.

Always check weather conditions and forecasts before you travel the trails. Again I will stress that you go prepared in every way you can, and be informed!

# Trail Etiquette

Let's face it, if you meet someone on the trail, they are there to have a good time and get away from it all, the same as you. If everyone exercises courtesy and cooperation, then everyone has a better time.

Trail etiquette also means having respect for the trail itself. Do not cut switchbacks on a trail. Switchbacks are built to make the trail easier, cutting them only makes your hike harder and causes erosion that damages the trail.

Downhill hikers must always yield to hikers coming uphill, and do it in such a way as to not break their stride or concentration.

If you are hiking faster than the party ahead of you, slow down and wait for them to allow you to pass at an ideal location; thank them.

If you stop for a rest, do so well off the trail, in order to give others a clear path to travel.

Do not hike or ride bikes on wet trails as this activity can cause permanent damage to the trails.

All trail users must yield to all trail stock. These animals can be excitable, and if you are not calm and quiet a rider (or even you) could be badly injured.

If you are allowed a pet on the trail, keep it on a leash. Be careful that you are clear of other hikers so the leash will not trip them.

Loud noises or yelling without reason is distracting to all. Allow others to enjoy the wilderness atmosphere without unnecessary noises.

If we all work together, we can make the great outdoors a pleasant place for everyone, now, as well as in the future.

# CONTENTS OF YOUR DAY PACK

Listed below are the items I feel comfortable with. Feel free to add or subtract to suit your needs. Keep in mind that you may be planning a day hike that could turninto an overnite stay for a variety of reasons. Go prepared!

1. Small flashlight, bulbs and batteries
2. Candies that will not melt or spoil
3. Whistle (a police whistle is ideal)
4. Good compass
5. Toilet paper
6. Complete first aid kit
7. Salt tablets
8. Strong sunscreen
9. Any medicines or prescriptions you require
10. Pocket knife
11. Pencil and paper
12. Lighter and waterproof matches
13. Moleskin
14. Lip salve
15. Bug spray for body
16. One day extra food that will not spoil
17. Leakproof canteen and extra water
18. Enough clothing for overnight stay if necessary
19. Plastic bag for litter
20. Raingear
21. Hat
22. Gloves or mittens
23. Sunglasses
24. Maps and Permits
25. Camera and film
26. Identification

I will stress that your maps are valuable only if you study them very carefully before you leave. Be sure you have chosen a hike that is correct for your capabilities.

Let your friends or family know where you are going, when you expect to return and then stick to that plan!

# CONTENTS OF YOUR BACKPACK

Backpacks are used primarily for multiple day outings. Be sure your pack is large enough and fits perfectly. Add the following items to your Day Pack List:

1. Sleeping bag and bed roll.
2. Tent
3. Camping stove and extra fuel.

# WHAT TO WEAR FOR MOUNTAIN HIKING

In the "Desert Survival" chapter in this book are hints on proper dress for the desert, but mountain dress has a different application. Mountain dress has its variables for lower rolling hills or higher rugged peaks.

## LOWER ROLLING HILLS

In these gentle areas, one can use with great comfort the lightweight hiking boots that are popular today. It's not too likely you will need extreme support for lower elevations. Most of these hikes are one-day outings or shorter, so a heavy backpack need not be carried making heavy footgear unnecessary.

Hiking shorts or denim pants work well here, as it is not likely to be cold. I prefer long sleeves and a hat to prevent sunburn. A day pack works well on shorter hikes of this nature. Sweat shirt and raingear are a must.

## HIGHER RUGGED PEAKS

In this kind of hiking one must have a very rugged hiking boot, not only for traction, but also for the ever-present need for good support. Some hikers even buy their boots a half size too large, making room for two pair of socks for more comfort. If you do not buy waterproof boots, then at least spray them with one of the products available to help them repel water.

Denim jeans wear well but do not provide much warmth in extreme cold. If you do wear them hiking, then consider carrying a warmer pair of pants and longjohns in case conditions turn colder. T-shirts are most comfortable under your outer shirts. Notice I said "shirts." I find wearing a couple of shirts instead of one heavy one makes it easier to adjust one's temperature by wearing only what is needed instead of too much or too little.

A warm hat, scarf and mittens and heavy jacket should also be carried on these hikes.

# WHAT TO DO WHEN YOU ARE LOST OR INJURED

You might think food, water, proper clothing, or even being attacked by wild animals are the most important concerns if you are lost in the wilderness.

However, all of the above are secondary or even immaterial if you do not exercise self-control. If you allow yourself to panic, then indeed you are lost and will probably only be found by accident. Understandably, this situation can instill fear, but do not give in to it!

Don't wander about. Sit down, relax and very carefully try to run through your mind the events that led up to your becoming lost.

If you fail to figure out what went wrong but you still have plenty of daylight left, travel slowly in the direction you feel is correct. Make sure that if you had been climbing that you now travel only downhill.

If you come to a stream, do not leave it unless, of course, you have found your trail. A stream can almost always supply you with water and food and usually leads to civilization as well.

Keep a very close eye on the daylight you have left. If your daylight will soon be gone, you should immediately find a place to camp overnight. Gather whatever rocks or stones are available, place them in a circle to make a place for a safe fire and gather a supply of wood. You should have a fire burning by the time it becomes dark, eaten whatever food you have allowed for your meal and know where everything in your camp is located.

If you cannot build a fire and do not have a blanket or bedroll, then cover yourself with sticks and leaves to escape the cold and wind; it works!

If you are injured and cannot travel, then a signal fire is your best bet. A very smoky fire by day and a bright fire at night has the best chance of bringing results. You can see how important the contents of your backpack or day pack can become.

Again, stay calm! Things can take a brighter outlook in the morning. It has been proven over and over that a clear head can get you out of almost any situation.

# Coping with Hypothermia

Hypothermia is a progressive physical and mental collapse that accompanies the cooling of the inner core of the body. It is the primary killer of outdoor recreationists. Symptoms include a feeling of being extremely cold, uncontrollable shivering and incoherent speech.

Getting wet in rain, sleet, snow or heavy fog or even perspiring, along with a moderately cool wind, can start the process at any time or altitude.

More than half your body's heat is lost from your head and neck being exposed. Obviously, then, a good winter hat with ear tabs, along with a scarf, will do a lot to slow down your major heat loss.

Other susceptible areas are your hands and feet. Mittens will keep you hands warmer than gloves, as the air around your hands will act as insulation. Waterproof boots will take care of your feet.

Some rain gear only drapes your upper body and allows your lower pant legs and boots to get soaking wet. A two-piece coat and pants set is better protection.

If you think that you or someone in your party may be suffering from hypothermia, get the person into dry clothes and get a fire started. It is most important to eat. Food will cause your body to develop heat from the digestion process. Administering warm drinks is also extremely beneficial.

If possible, get the person into a prewarmed sleeping bag heated either at your fire or by having someone lie down in it. Build an insulation barrier with leaves, etc., on which to lay the sleeping bag and to keep it out of the wind.

If the patient is going into severe hypothermia, strip him and yourself of clothing and get into the sleeping bag together. There is no faster way to convey body heat.

When planning a hike, think hypothermia. When shopping for hiking gear, when planning your backpack or day pack, think hypothermia!

# SAFETY RULES FOR SURVIVAL IN THE DESERT

*(Courtesy Maricopa County Civil Defense and Emergency Services)*

1. Never go into the desert without first informing someone as to your destination, your route and when you will return. STICK TO YOUR PLAN.

2. Carry at least one gallon of water per person per day of your trip. Plastic jugs are handy and portable.

3. Be sure your vehicle is in good condition.

4. KEEP AN EYE ON THE SKY. Flash floods may occur any time "thunderheads" are in sight, even though it may not rain where you are.

5. If your vehicle breaks down, stay near it. Your emergency supplies are here. Raise your hood and trunk lid to denote "Help Needed"

6. If you are POSITIVE of the route to help, and must leave your vehicle, leave a note for rescuers as to when you left and the direction you are taking.

7. If you have water — DRINK IT. Do not ration it.

8. If water is limited — KEEP YOUR MOUTH SHUT. Do not talk, do not eat, do not smoke, do not drink alcohol, do not take salt.

9. Do not sit or lie DIRECTLY on the ground. It may be 30 degrees or more hotter than the air.

10. A roadway is a sign of civilization. IF YOU FIND A ROAD, STAY ON IT.

The Desert Southwest is characterized by brilliant sunshine, a wide temperature range, sparse vegetation, a scarcity of water, a high rate of evaporation and low annual rainfall.

Travel in the desert can be an interesting and enjoyable experience or it can be a fatal or near fatal nightmare. The contents of this manual can give only a few of the details necessary for full enjoyment of our desert out-of-doors.

If you think you are lost, do not panic. Sit down for a while, survey the area and take stock of the situation. Try to remember how long it has been since you knew where you were. Decide on a course of action. It may be best to stay right where you are and let your companions or rescuers look for you. This is especially true if there is water and fuel nearby or if there is some means of shelter. Once you decide to remain, make a fire — a smoky one for daytime and a bright one for the night. Other signals may be used, but fire is by far the best.

REMEMBER, MOVE WITH A PURPOSE, NEVER START OUT AND WANDER AIMLESSLY.

**Walking:** There are special rules and techniques for walking in the desert. By walking slowly and resting about 10 minutes per hour a man in good physical condition can cover about 12-18 miles per day — less after he becomes fatigued or lacks sufficient water or food. On the hot desert it is best to travel early morning or late evening, spending mid-day in whatever shade may be available. In walking, pick the easiest and safest way. Go around obstacles, not over them. Instead of going up or down steep slopes, zigzag to prevent undue exertion. Go around gullies and canyons instead of through them. When walking with companions, adjust the rate to the slowest man. Keep together but allow about 10 feet between members.

At rest stops, if you can sit down in the shade and prop your feet up, remove your shoes and change socks, or straighten out the ones you are wearing. If the ground is too hot to sit on, no shade is available, and you cannot raise your feet, do not remove your shoes as you may not be able to get them back onto swollen feet.

**Automobile Driving:** Cross country driving or driving on little used roads is hazardous, but can be done successfully if a few simple rules are followed. Move slowly. Do not attempt to negotiate washes without first checking the footing and the clearances. High centers may rupture the oil pan. Overhang may cause the driving wheels to become suspended above the ground. Do not spin wheels in an attempt to gain motion, but apply power very slowly to prevent wheel spin and subsequent digging in. When driving in sand, traction can be increased by partially deflating tires. Start, stop and turn gradually, as sudden motions cause wheels to dig in. There are certain tool and equipment requirements if you intend to drive off the main roads: a shovel, a pick-mattock, a tow chain or cable, at least 50 feet of strong tow rope, tire pump, axe, water cans, gas cans, and of course, your regular spare parts and auto tools.

**Clothing:** For the desert, light-weight and light colored clothing which covers the whole body is best. Long trousers and long sleeves protect from the sun, help to prevent dehydration and protect against insects, abrasions and lacerations by rocks and brush. Headgear should provide all-around shade as well as eye shade.

**Survival Kit:** Items that should be carried on the individual are: a sharp knife, a signal mirror, a map of the area, thirty or more feet of nylon string, canteen, matches, a snake bite kit, a firearm and ammunition, and other items that may be useful. Consider carrying your gear in a small rucksack or pack over your shoulders. Weight carried in this manner is less tiring than if carried in pockets or hung on the belt. The pack can be used to sit upon. It also affords a safer method of carrying items, such as the belt knife, hatchet, etc., which may lend to the chances of injury in case of a fall.

**Health Hazards:** Thought must be given to protecting your health and well-being, and the prevention of fatigue and injury: first, because medical assistance will be some distance away; second, because conditions are usually different and distinct from your everyday living. The desert is a usually healthy environment due to dryness, the lack of human and animal wastes, and the sterilizing effect of the hot sun. Therefore, your immediate bodily needs will be your first consideration.

If you are walking or active, rest 10 minutes each hour. Drink plenty of water, especially early in the morning while the temperature is still low.

While in the desert, wear sun glasses to protect your eyes from glare. Even though the glare does not seem to bother you, it will impair your distant vision and will retard your adaptation to night conditions. If you have no glasses make an eyeshade by slitting a piece of paper, cardboard or cloth. Applying charcoal or soot around the eyes is also beneficial.

In a survival situation everything that you do, each motion that you make, and each step you take must be preceded by the thought: am I safe in doing this?

Keep your clothing on, including shirt and hat. Clothing helps ration your sweat by slowing the evaporation rate and prolonging the cooling effect. It also keeps out the hot desert air and reflects the heat of the sun.

Rationing water at high temperatures is actually inviting disaster because small amounts will not prevent dehydration. Loss of efficiency and collapse always follows dehydration. It is the water in your body that maintains your life, not the water in your canteen.

Keep the mouth shut and breathe through the nose to reduce water loss and drying of mucous membranes. Avoid conversation for the same reason. If possible, cover lips with grease or oil. Alcohol in any form is to be avoided as it will accelerate dehydration. Consider alcohol as food and not as water since additional water is required to assimilate the alcohol. For the same reason, food intake should be kept to a minimum if sufficient water is not available.

**Carrying Water:** When planning to travel, give your water supply extra thought. Do not carry water in glass containers as these may break. Metal insulated containers are good, but heavy. Carry some water in gallon or half-gallon plastic containers similar to those containing bleach. They are unbreakable, light-weight and carrying several will assure a water supply if one is damaged.

**Finding Water in the Desert:** If you are near water it is best to remain there and prepare signals for your rescuers. If no water is immediately available look for it, following these leads:

Watch for desert trails — following them may lead to water or civilization, particularly if several such trails join and point toward a specific location.

Flocks of birds will circle over water holes. Listen for their chirping in the morning and evening, and you may be able to locate their watering spot. Quail move toward water in the late afternoon and away in the morning. Doves flock toward watering spots morning and evening. Also look for indications of animals as they tend to feed near water.

Look for plants which grow only where there is water: cottonwoods, sycamores, willows, hackberry, saltcedar, cattails and arrow weed. You may have to dig to find this water. Also keep on the lookout for windmills and water tanks built by ranchers. If cactus fruits are ripe, eat a lot of them to help prevent dehydration.

**Methods of Purifying Water:** Dirty water should be filtered through several layers of cloth or allowed to settle. This does not purify the water even though it may look clean. Purification to kill germs must be done by one of the following methods:

1. Water purification tablets are the easiest to use. Get them from the drug store and follow the directions on the label. Let stand for thirty minutes.

2. Tincture of Iodine: add three drops per quart of clear water, double for cloudy water. Let stand for thirty minutes.

3. Boiling for 3 to 5 minutes will purify most water.

**Food:** You must have water to survive, but you can go without food for a few days without harmful effects. In fact, if water is not available, do not eat, as food will only increase your need for water. The important thing about locating food in a survival situation is to know what foods are available in the particular invironment and how to obtain them. Hawks soaring overhead may mean water is nearby. Game will be found around water holes and areas that have heavy brush growth.

**Edible Wildlife:** Almost every animal, reptile and insect is edible. Learn how to prepare the various things that would be available to you in a survival situation. Avoid any small mammal which appears to be sick. Some animals have scent glands which must be removed before cooking. Do not allow the animal hair to come in contact with the flesh as it will give the meat a disagreeable taste.

1. Jack Rabbit: A hare, with long ears and legs, sandy color. Grubs are often found in the hide or flesh but these do not affect the food value.

2. Cottontail Rabbit: Small, pale gray with white tail. Active in the early morning and late evening.

3. Javelina: Dark gray-black, weighing 30-50 pounds with strong tusks. Has scent glands on the back, over the hind legs. May be dangerous if cornered or wounded.

4. Mourning Dove: Year-round resident, usually found near habitation and water.

5. Gambel's Quail, Scaled Quail, Mearn's Quail: The Gambel's is of primary importance in desert and semi-arid areas.

6. Snakes: Most snakes are edible. Rattlesnake is especially good.

7. Desert Tortoise.

**Edible Plants:** The main desert edibles are the fruits of the cacti and legumes. All cactus fruits are safe to eat. In the summer the fleshy and thin-walled ripe fruits can be singed over a fire to remove spines. Then they can be peeled and eaten. Old cactus fruits contain seeds which can be pounded between two stones into a powder and eaten, or mixed with water into a gruel. New, young pads of the prickly pear can be singed, peeled and boiled.

The legumes are the bean bearing plants. The main ones are the mesquite, the palo verde, the ironwood and the catclaw. All are small trees with fern-like leaves. All have bean pods which when green and tender can be boiled and eaten. Dry, mature beans, like cactus seeds, are too hard to chew and must be cooked.

In a survival situation, where the use of strange plants for food is indicated, follow these rules: Avoid plants with milky sap. Avoid all red beans. If possible, boil plants which are questionable. Test a cooked plant by holding a small quantity in the mouth for a few moments. If the taste is disagreeable, do not eat it.

**Fires and Cooking:** Clear an area about 15 feet across, dig a pit or arrange rocks to contain the fire. Make a starting fire of dry grass, small twigs, shavings, under-bark of cottonwoods, etc. Place larger twigs — about pencil size — on top. Have heavier material ready to add, using the small pieces first. Place them on the fire in a "tepee" fashion to prevent smothering your starting fire and aid in the formation of an up-draft. After the fire is burning well, continue to use the tepee method for boiling but criss-cross fuel for forming coals for frying or broiling.

Start your fire with a lighter, matches, or a hand lens. Remember, do not use up your water-proofed matches unless your return from the field is a guaranteed fact. Here are some hints for expeditious fire building.

Drying matches: Damp wooden matches can be dried by stroking 20 to 30 times through the dry hair at the side of the head. Be careful not to knock off the chemical head of very wet matches at the start of the procedure.

Tinder: (All of these must be dry.) Under-bark of the cottonwood, cedar bark, dead goldenrod tops, cattail floss, charred cloth, bird nests, mouse nests, or any readily flammable material shredded into fine fibers.

Fuzz-stick: Cut slivers into soft wood sticks and arrange them tepee fashion with the separated ends downward.

Quick, hot fires: Cottonwood, cactus skeletons, creosote-bush, aspen, tamarisk, cedar, pine, and spruce.

Long-lasting fires: Mesquite, ironwood, black jack, sage, and oak.

REMEMBER, YOU WANT FLAME FOR HEAT, EMBERS FOR COOKING, AND FOR SIGNALS YOU NEED SMOKE IN THE DAYTIME AND BRIGHT FIRES AT NIGHT. BE SURE TO EXTINGUISH YOUR FIRE BEFORE LEAVING IT!

**Poisonous Creatures:** There is probably more said and less truth about poisonous creatures than any other subject. These animals and insects are for the most part shy, or due to their nature, not often seen. Learn the facts about these creatures and you will see that they are not to be feared but only respected.

Snakes: There are many types of snakes in the southwest but only rattlesnakes and coral snakes are poisonous. Snakes hibernate during the colder months, but will start appearing with the warming trend, sometimes in early February. During the spring and fall months they may be found out in the daytime, but during the summer months they will generally be found out during the night, due to the fact that they cannot stand excessive heat.

Rattlesnakes: These are easily identified by the sandy color, the broad arrow-shaped head, blunt tipped-up nose, and rattles on the tail. Look for them mostly where food, water, and protection is available — around abandoned structures, irrigation ditches, water holes, brush and rock piles. They do not always give warning by rattling, nor do they always strike if one is close. If travelling in areas where rattlers are, wear protective footgear and watch where you put your hands and feet.

Arizona Coral Snake: A small snake, rarely over 20 inches long with small blunt, black head and tapering tail. Wide red and black bands are separated by narrower yellow bands and all completely encircle the body. They are noctunal and live under objects, in burrows, and are shy and timid. Corals bite and chew rather than strike, but due to the very small mouth they are unable to bite any but the smallest extremities.

Treatment of Poisonous Snakebite: If bitten, try to capture the snake as identification will aid in specific medical treatment.

1. KEEP THE VICTIM QUIET AND SEEK MEDICAL HELP.

2. If the "cut and suck" method is deemed necessary, follow the instructions with the snake bite kit. In any event, step 1 above, is very important.

Poisonous Insects and Spiders: The potentially lethal species in this area are the scorpion and the black widow spider.

Prevention and Treatment: In places where venomous species are expected, inspect all clothing and bedding before use, especially items that have been on or near the ground. If bitten (stung), get to a doctor, especially if the victim is a child, is elderly, has a bad heart, or has been bitten several times or on the main part of the body.

# Index

## A — F

**Abbey's Way Trail #151**  72
Alder Creek Trail  50
Alpine, AZ  24, 26, 30
Amethyst Mine  46
**Amethyst Trail #253**  44, 46, 48
Apache Junction, AZ  52, 92
Armer Mountain  78, 96
Aztec Peak  72, 76, 78, 80
**Babe Haught Trail #143**  56
Bartlett Lake  14
**Bear Canyon Trail #299**  82, 88, 90
Bear Valley Trail #55  28
Black Bear Saddle  50
**Black Mesa Trail #241**  92, 94
Blue Ridge Primitive Area  30
Blue River Trail #101  30, 32
Boulder Canyon  94
Brown's Saddle  44, 46, 48
**Brown's Trail #133**  46
Buckhorn Mountain  48, 50
Buckhorn Ridge  48, 50
Campaign Creek  98
Campaign Trail #256  98
Campbell Flat Trail #54  28
Cave Creek  20
**Cave Creek Tr. #4**  12, 16, 20, 22
CCC Campground  12
Chalk Canyon  12
Chillicut Trail  50
Chitty Creek  26
Chitty Trail #37  26
Cinch Hook Butte  68
Claypool, AZ  76, 78
Cold Springs Canyon  76, 80
Cottonwood Creek  20
Cottonwood Trail #247  12, 18, 20, 22
Crabtree Creek  26
Crabtree Trail #22  24, 26

Cramm Mtn. mining operation  22
**Dan's Trail #550**  74
Derrick Trail #33  64
Dog House Spring  34, 42
Dripping Springs  68
Dry Prong Creek  24
Dry Prong Trail #45  26
Dude Fire  60
Dutch Henry Trail #297  82
**Dutchman's Trail #104**  92, 94
Eagle Canyon  24
East Eagle Creek  26
**East Eagle Trail #33**  24
Edwards Spring  80
Ferndell Spring  38
First Water Creek  94
**Four Peaks Trail #130**  44, 46, 48, 50, 54
Four Peaks Wilderness area  78
Freemont Saddle  52
**Frye Canyon Trail #36**  84
Frye Creek  84
Frye Mesa  84

## G — M

Garden Valley  92
Gila Topminnow  12
Glenwood, NM  28
Globe, AZ  34, 38
Granite Springs  50
**Grant Goudy Ridge Tr. #310**  86
Granville, AZ  32
Greasewood Mountains  86, 90
Grey, Zane  64
Hackberry Creek  50
Hagan Trail #31  32
Haught, Anderson Lee "Babe"  56
Helispot 166, 167  26
**Highline Trail #31**  58, 64, 68, 70
**Highline Trail #47**  26
Horton Creek  62, 64
**Horton Creek Trail #285**  62

Horton Spring Trail #292.  64
Hot Air Trail #15   24
Humboldt Mountain   12, 22
Hunt Spring   80
**Icehouse Canyon Trail #198**
   34, 36, 38, 42
Inception junction   84
Jacobson Ridge   88
**Jug Trail #61**   96
Kellner Canyon Spring   36
Kellner Canyon Trail #242 34, 36, 40
Ladybug Saddle   82, 90
**Ladybug Trail #329**   82, 88
Lengthy Trail #89   32
**Little Blue Creek Trail #41**   28
Lone Pine Saddle   46, 48, 54
Matty's Fork drainage   12, 18
Maverick Mountain   14
McBride Mesa Trail #26   26
Miami, AZ   80
Moody Point Trail   80
Mt. Graham   84
Murphy Ranch   80
**Murphy Ranch Trail #141** 76, 80

**N — T**

New River Mesa   16, 20, 22
Oak Flat Trail #123   48
**Palo Verde Trail #512**   14
**Parker Creek Trail #160**   78
Parker Pass   94
Parsnip Springs   68
Payson, AZ   46, 56, 58
**Peralta Trail #102**   52
Pigeon Spring   54
**Pigeon Trail #134**   54
Pinal Campgrounds   40
Pinal Mtns   34, 36, 38, 40, 42
Piñaleno Mountains   82, 88, 90
Pine, AZ   66
**Pine Canyon Trail #26**   66
Pine Trailhead   60, 66
Pinyon Camp   52

Pioneer Basin   40
Pioneer Pass Trailhead   40
Promontory Butte Trail #278   64
Quien Sabe Spring   18, 22
**Quien Sabe Trail #250** 12, 16, 20, 22
Raspberry Creek   30
**Raspberry Trail #35**   30
Rattlesnake Cove   14
Rattlesnake Ranch   30
**Reavis Gap Trail #117**   98
Reavis Ranch   98
**Rim Trail #139**   76, 78, 80
Roosevelt Lake   78, 96
Rose Peak fire tower   32
Round-The-Mtn. Trail #302  84

**S — Z**

Safford, AZ   82
Salome Creek   96
Salome Wilderness   96
Salthouse Creek   26
Salthouse Trail #18   24, 26
San Francisco River   28
Saunders cabin   26
SB Cove   14
Schall Canyon   68
Second Water Trail #236   92
**See Canyon Trail #184**   70
See Spring   70
Seven Springs Rec. Area  12, 16, 20, 22
Shake Springs   48
**Shake Trail #309**   90
Sierra Ancha Exp. Forest   78
Sierra Ancha Wilderness   76
Sixshooter Canyon   34
**Sixshooter Canyon Trail #197**
   36, 38, 42
**Skull Mesa Trail #248**   16, 20
**Skunk Tank Trail #246** 16, 18, 22
Soldier Creek Campground   86
Spradling Canyon   68
Spur Cross trailhead   16, 20

Squaw Spring Trail #196  40
Squirrel Trail #34   26
Stockton Pass    90
**Strayhorse Canyon Trail #20**  32
Stockton Pass Campground  90
Strayhorse Campground  24, 26, 30
Sulpher Springs Valley   86, 90
Superstition Mountains   52, 92, 94, 98, 100
**Telephone Trail #192**  34, 38, 42

Thatcher, AZ   84
Tonto Basin    48
Tonto Creek    64
Tonto National Forest   12, 22
Tule Canyon    100
**Tule Canyon Trail #122**   100
Two Bar Ridge Trail #119  98, 100
Weaver's Needle    52, 92
Woods Canyon Lake    70
Workman Falls    80

## About the Artist

Robyn Wasserman graduated with degrees in Forest Recreation and Natural Resource Management.  She has resided in Arizona for 14 years and worked as a park naturalist, hiking guide, fire dispatcher, nursery caretaker and tour guide.

Currently living in Southern Arizona, Robyn is employed as a ranger with Arizona State Parks.  When not working, she enjoys hiking, reading, gardening, photography, nature crafts and spending time with her friends.

# About the Author

With a degree in Wildlife/Forestry Conservation, it is not surprising that Don Kiefer spends as much time as possible outdoors. Don's books share his experiences and practical knowledge of hiking Arizona. He has done volunteer work with the National Park Service, recording over 500 hours in the Rincon Wilderness looking for those needing help. The National Forest Service, Pima County Parklands Foundation and Arizona State Parks have also benefitted from Don's services. He has logged over 1,000 hiking miles as a member of the Prevention Walking Society, and an overall total of 4,000 miles of hiking throughout Arizona.

Having learned to fly, Don is especially proud to be an honorary member of the 161st Air Refueling Group at Sky Harbor Airport.

Don began sharing his outdoor world when he started writing for the *Mesa Tribune*. He has now completed five hiking books on Arizona. At the same time, he has been working hard on a hiking library of his own which already consists of 42 volumes, and when complete, will cover every trail in the state.

Don has been cited twice by the National Forest Service and as many times by the National Park Service. He has been honored by B. Dalton Booksellers, as well as Senator John McCain, for his willingness to share his world and his time with everyone. On the wall of Don's office is the Presidential Sports Award received from President George Bush in 1991.

Don is currently working on new hiking books and a book about "haunted" Arizona.

## SNAKES and other REPTILES of the SOUTHWEST

This book is a must for hikers, hunters, campers and all outdoor enthusiasts! More than 80 photographs and illustrations in the text and full color plate insert, this book is the definitive, easy-to-use guide to Southwestern reptiles! By Erik Stoops and Annette Wright.

6 x 9 — 128 Pages . . . $9.95

## SCORPIONS and VENOMOUS INSECTS of the SOUTHWEST

A user-friendly guide to the wide variety of scorpions and other venomous creatures of the Southwest. Scorpions, spiders, ticks and mites, centipedes, millipedes, bees and more are shown in detailed illustrations and full color photos. By Erik Stoops and Jeffrey Martin.

5 1/2 x 8 1/2 — 112 Pages . . . $9.95

## EXPLORE ARIZONA!

Where to find old coins, bottles, fossil beds, arrowheads, petroglyphs, waterfalls, ice caves, cliff dwellings. Detailed maps to 59 Arizona wonders! By Rick Harris.

5 1/2 x 8 1/2 — 128 pages . . . $6.95

## DISCOVER ARIZONA!

Enjoy the thrill of discovery! Prehistoric ruins, historic battlegrounds, fossil beds, arrowheads, rock crystals and semi-precious stones! By Rick Harris.

5 1/2 x 8 1/2 — 112 Pages . . . $6.95

## HORSE TRAILS IN ARIZONA

Complete guide to over 100 of Arizona's most beautiful equestrian trails, from the desert to the high country. Maps, directions to trailheads, water availability and more to ensure an unmatched experience for all who love hoseback riding. Lodging and "hitchin' post" restaurant information, too! By Jan Hancock.

(Revised 1998 Edition)    5 1/2 x 8 1/2 — 160 Pages . . . $12.95